CREATIVE ENTREPRENEURSHIP
On A Smaller Scale

Stories and Strategies of
Entrepreneurship in Action

WALTER BAKER

This book is dedicated to my late wife, Barbara
She was the loving heart of our family
And a steadfast support to our ventures together

Acknowledgements

Over the course of my professional life, I have worked with, learned from and been inspired by many, many people in universities, public service and those who joined with me in my entrepreneurial ventures. Some of them are mentioned in this book. I would also like to thank my long-time collaborator, Anne Perkins, for her role as a sounding board, researcher and editor in the preparation of a manuscript that has evolved over several years. Finally, as always, I would like to acknowledge the support, encouragement, and assistance from members of my family – children and grandchildren and their spouses – that were essential for turning this particular vision into reality.

Walter Baker
August 2020

Foreword

Entrepreneurs are organization-builders. If you are already an entrepreneur, or will become one in the future, you will be part of a growing community of those who focus creative and innovative strengths on building new organizations they believe are needed. For every Bill Gates and Richard Branson, there are a great many entrepreneurs working on a smaller scale. Society needs us. We build many new organizations to meet an ever-growing and rapidly changing demand for goods and services. In doing so, we create jobs vital to the economy and to the vast majority of those in the population who look to organizations for their work.

Intrapreneurs are a special kind of entrepreneur. Rather than drawing on their entrepreneurial strengths and skills to create new organizations, they apply such strengths within existing organizations to help effective innovations meet identified internal needs. Organizations need to adapt to shifting circumstances. Many begin to take on a form and direction quite different from what was initially intended. Add to this the complicating factor of today's turbulent environment which strengthens the need for intrapreneurs in existing organizations to help them grow, reorganize, revitalize, or evolve into something different. As with entrepreneurs, for every organizational transformation led by an intrapreneur of exceptional ability, there are very many intrapreneurs working on a smaller scale who apply their talents usefully to organizational innovations.

The book is, to a considerable extent, autobiographical. Using a series of thirteen stories, I work my way through an entrepreneurial career that began at the age of 17 with a used bicycle business and progressed through ever-more-challenging ventures. From time to time, my entrepreneurial activities are situated in life outside entrepreneurship to illustrate the interaction between entrepreneurship and other vital activities in our lives. In adopting this approach, the aim is to bring entrepreneurship alive from the perspective of someone who has experienced both the joys and special challenges of life as a creative entrepreneur and gained great pleasure and personal satisfaction from its exercise.

It is my hope that the following stories will be of interest to those who are already entrepreneurs, those who want to learn more about entrepreneurship and its role in society whether they hope to be entrepreneurs or simply want to learn about it, as well as to the growing body of educators now working with aspiring or practising entrepreneurs. Each story is followed by commentary and a list of questions for the reader to consider.

There are eight chapters to the book. Chapter One introduces the concept and practice of *creative entrepreneurship* as a vital role in society through three short stories. Chapter Two focuses on *entrepreneurship-in-action* with stories about the creation of three different organizations and what was learned from these experiences. Chapter Three has three stories about *intrapreneurship-in-action* and discusses the special challenges when creative entrepreneurship is practiced within existing organizations. Chapter Four is written around three interrelated stories about exploring, acquiring and developing Strathmere as a family business and identifies several key elements of the entrepreneurial process. Chapter Five reflects on the performance factors, strengths and commitment of entrepreneurs and entrepreneurial attributes are identified with the entrepreneurial mind and spirit. The chapter also includes a self-assessment questionnaire. Chapter Six asks if entrepreneurship is or should be a profession, and examines key factors that support and enrich it. Chapter Seven reflects on how entrepreneurial strategies are based on my experiences. Chapter Eight contains a final story and concluding thoughts about the nature of entrepreneurship.

Three appendices are also included. The first sets out the milestones in my career to assist the reader in situating the entrepreneurial and intrapreneurial ventures described in the stories in the context of my broader professional life. The second is a self-assessment questionnaire for the reader to record personal scores and comments. The third provides further references related to entrepreneurship issues that the reader might wish to review.

CONTENTS

CHAPTER ONE
The Nature of Entrepreneurship

This chapter introduces key themes through three short stories.

1. How, under specific circumstances, "necessity is the mother of invention" in sparking a new entrepreneurial venture.
2. The concept of "creative entrepreneurship", why the term "creative" is so important, and how "innovation" is the essential com-plement to creativity in entrepreneurship
3. The vital role entrepreneurs play in the business sector and the critical, if less well-known, role they play in the public sector, the not-for-profit sector, and society-at-large

Story One: Building a Used Bicycle Business

My first venture into entrepreneurship was on a very small scale. I was 17 and newly enrolled at St. John's College, York in northern England, in a two-year program designed to prepare me for a teaching career. Although tuition and room and board were provided by a benevolent British government, it was up to each student to finance incidentals that went along with a college education.

As the son of working class parents, there were no family savings on which to draw and any money generated from my own part-time work was contributed to family funds. In those days, there was no access to student loans. St. John's students were also prohibited from taking part-time employment because of the demanding nature of the program.

The Story

During my early teens I had purchased, repaired and sold a number of used bicycles, and had taken my bicycle and tools to college with me. Many students had bicycles and those who did not soon learned how useful they were for travelling around York. Accordingly, I found space to work in a secluded corner of the campus and shortly after arriving was operating a used bicycle business.

Students needing repairs to their bicycles provided up-front cash to purchase the required parts. What they paid for in repairs and used bicycle purchases was enough to keep me in incidentals throughout the two years I operated the business. I left college with my bicycle and a somewhat better set of tools. That was the end of my entrepreneurial activities for the next four years.

Although the used bicycle venture was small, it taught me something about being an entrepreneur. I can recall vividly the first occasion the college principal passed by as I was busy repairing a bicycle, with tools and spare parts spread around me. He paused, looking slightly bemused, as if wondering whether I should be there and if, perhaps, there was some college rule being broken. I greeted him cheerfully, introduced myself, told him what I was doing and why, and watched with relief as he continued on his way with a nod that signified I had his approval to continue.

Commentary

1. I must have known intuitively what entrepreneurs generally learn at some point — that it is easier at times to gain approval for something on which we are already embarked than to gain permission for it in advance.
2. I learned, also, that a small entrepreneurial venture could be started without capital when the need for the service was genuine and could be self-financing.
3. Entrepreneurial opportunities are plentiful in modern societies. Over many

centuries, we have learned how to come together into organizations of differing sizes and varieties, each emerging to serve needs their creators have identified.

4. Among such organizations are those built by entrepreneurs, distinguished by their existence outside existing organizational society.

5. The entrepreneur's world is dynamic. Existing organizations die off. New ones emerge. Those surviving over time go through larger or smaller transformations. As society-at-large goes through its own rich and challenging changes, new needs arise to be met and new entrepreneurial niches need to be filled. Involved in such organizational change are entrepreneurs and intrapreneurs as creators and transformers of the organizations on which we have grown to depend so irreversibly.

Story Two: Entrepreneurship, Creativity and Innovation

A key feature of entrepreneurship is the especially creative nature of challenging endeavors and how creativity, when exercised in conjunction with innovative capacity, transforms entrepreneurship into an art and craft comparable to the work of creative artists and craftsmen.

The Story

I once built a private school, day camp, riding stable and family recreation program called Echo Park in Bloomfield Hills, Michigan. It originated quite by chance. A friend I was visiting in Pontiac drove me through Bloomfield Hills to show me what he regarded as a most attractive community of wealthy young families where he hoped one day to live.

The area struck me as a great place in which to build an upscale version of a private school and camp I had built earlier in Toronto, Ontario. I was totally without capital at the time, and such an idea might well have been discarded as not worth a second thought. Yet, it took root.

For weeks I commuted between Toronto and Bloomfield Hills, spending roughly three days a week on the project until I became convinced it was a feasible venture worth pursuing. Over the next two years, I raised from individuals in the community the capital needed to buy and renovate a 26-room mansion on 92 acres of land in the heart of Bloomfield Hills, and led the building of what existed originally only in my mind's eye.

In the process I met one of Michigan's finest portrait painters and sculptors, John Coppin, whose home and studio were on land next to our project. After he showed me his impressive paintings and sculptures, I said, "John, it must be wonderful to be so creative!" He responded, "I have been watching you convert that white elephant of a property into an attractive nursery school and camp and thinking to myself, "It must be wonderful to be so creative!"

John saw through his artist's eye that where he created with oils and clay, we were using as our own creative media the materials of which organizations are made. Challenging entrepreneurial ventures are very much exercises in creativity and innovation.

An expanded version of the Echo Park story appears at the end of Chapter 2.

Commentary

1. If you have the mind-set, spirit and skills of an entrepreneur, there could be challenges awaiting you in every sector.
6. The creative insights acquired by current entrepreneurs and their predecessors throughout history in response to entrepreneurial challenges and opportunities are relatively few compared to the number of entrepreneurial insights still waiting to be obtained or which will emerge in our turbulent, rapidly changing environments.

Story Three: John J. Kelso - Entrepreneurship beyond the Business Sector

Although the term "entrepreneur" is currently used most frequently in relation to the business world, entrepreneurs are needed and active in every sector of society. Each sector has its own needs and related organizations, and is heavily dependent on how well these organizations are built and function in their unique environments.

The Story

Early in my career, I worked with children's aid societies to support my university studies. I became familiar with the work of John J. Kelso, a superb creative entrepreneur who was active in the social service sector in the 1800s. Kelso was a Toronto reporter whose special territory was the law courts Day after day he would see neglected and abused street children being brought before a magistrate for some misdemeanor. At the time, there was no legislation or institutional provisions protecting children from parental neglect, abuse or abandonment.

Kelso was so moved by the plight of such children that he founded the first children's aid society and went on to lobby successfully for a new child protection statute. He became Ontario's Superintendent of Neglected and Dependent Children and over the next several years was the driving force behind setting up a network of 55 private children's aid societies across Ontario. He then went on to lead or support child welfare initiatives across Canada and the northern United States.

Commentary

2. Entrepreneurs like John Kelso have created many other not-for-profit organizations. Together, these organizations form an important part of an active non-profit sector in which the creative entrepreneur who launches a "Habitat for Humanity" movement in response to a crucial need for housing for the economically disadvantaged, or develops a series of food banks to help poverty-stricken families meet the most basic need for food, might well experience the same challenges and creative satisfaction as that of the successful business entrepreneur.

7. The public service sector is also fertile ground for entrepreneurship (as well as intrapreneurship). Its organizations are in a state of continuous change, and the stereotype of the large bureaucratic department with its focus on permanence and routine is somewhat removed from the reality of today's public sector organizations.

8. What Kelso engaged in was only one of many entrepreneurial initiatives taking place in federal, provincial and local governments across Canada and,

indeed, across developed and developing worlds. Unlike the opportunities in the business sector, public sector opportunities are not normally of a profit–making nature. They can be of great social value, nonetheless, as the following quotation from Tidd and Bessant describes:

> "Public sector entrepreneurship ventures may not generate profits but do affect the quality of life for millions of people. Bright ideas well implemented can lead to valued new services and the efficient delivery of existing ones... New ideas have the potential to change the quality of life and the availability of opportunity for people in some of the poorest regions of the world."

> There is plenty of scope for innovation and entrepreneurship ***and at the limit we are talking of life and death***". (Managing Innovation: Integrating Technological, Market and Organizational Change, 2013)

CHAPTER TWO
Entrepreneurship-in-Action

There are three stories in this chapter:

- Courier School Bus Company
- Glendon Park Nursery School and Day Camp
- Echo Park

They are interlinked and illustrate how one entrepreneurial venture can lead to another and then to still others. All three focus on the business sector.

Story Four: Courier School Bus Company

This is a case of entrepreneurship at its most basic. It illustrates how a small business grew from familiarity with an existing nursery school which faced financial problems threatening its survival. Helping to resolve such problems led to my becoming involved in the business affairs of the school.

This involvement, in turn, led to awareness of a transportation need I would not otherwise have recognized.

Recognition of the need for better transportation was the entrepreneurial trigger. Resolving this need led to the recognition of a broader need in the outside community which, once addressed, resulted in the emergence of a school bus company and its subsequent expansion to incorporate parcel delivery and messenger services.

There was nothing spectacular about building a small school bus company. It did, however, require functioning as a creative entrepreneur on a smaller scale.

The Story

What led me into entrepreneurship after my used bicycle business and subsequent years as a university student were the terms of a fellowship I had been awarded to study for a doctorate. Under such terms I was not permitted to take a part-time job outside the university to supplement the modest fellowship income, although I was allowed to teach a university course.

Previously, I had combined the demands of a university education with the special demands of working in parallel to generate the income we needed as a family. It proved harder than I had foreseen to be, for the first time, a full-time student. To give more balance to my life, I became the President of my son David's nursery school.

David was then three years old. Because my wife Barbara worked part-time, we enrolled him in the nursery school, located in a large old house with a playground for outdoor activities. Three months into the school year, parents were asked to attend an emergency meeting where we learned that the school was about to be moved to a different, far less attractive location. The reason given was that enrolment was insufficient to finance the school at its current site.

Such a move would have been disruptive for the children generally. For our family it would have meant new transportation costs we would have been hard-pressed to meet. Accordingly, I volunteered to head a small group of parents to work on raising the enrolment and addressing the financial challenges more generally. We were successful in this, and the school stayed where it was. I took on the role of President and was given the use of a small apartment above the school in exchange for watching over the school's management affairs.

Once I understood how the school functioned, it became clear that it was in need of better transportation. Children were being moved to and from school by taxi. The taxi drivers, understandably, tried to fit their school trips around their other calls, and even the most conscientious drivers were caught on occasion too far away from their nursery school pick-ups to arrive on time.

Anyone who has dressed children for nursery school, and required them to wait patiently for a taxi that does not arrive when scheduled, will know how their willingness to go to school could lessen to the point where there was no alternative but to let them stay home.

Accordingly, I recommended to the Board that we acquire a small school bus and transport the children ourselves. Having only recently survived a financial crisis, the Board was understandably reluctant to take on new debt, even while agreeing that the taxi option was not working well and that improved transportation would have a positive effect on enrolment.

They did agree, however, that it was acceptable that I buy the bus and have the school's janitor, Vinco, obtain the qualifications to drive it. Vinco had been with the school a number of years, had children of his own, was popular with the students, had the time to spare and was, therefore, ideal as the driver.

When I went to the bank to seek to borrow the money to buy a vehicle, armed with a short business case to show financial feasibility, the Bank Manager was away for a few days. He had left an eager Assistant Bank Manager in charge who proved to be receptive to my proposal. I walked away with the funds to buy a nine-passenger station wagon that was suitable in those pre-seatbelt days for transporting 12 nursery school students in safety and comfort. Vinco qualified himself as the driver and made four trips a day. We were able to charge parents a lower fee than the cost of taxi service and still generate a modest profit.

Without being aware of it, I had taken the first step toward founding a school bus company. It turned out that the need for better transportation existed in other nursery and primary schools across the city. As schools learned of our existence, they began to call and request that we provide service to them. I had stumbled on a promising market niche in which to operate and within a year had six 12-passenger vehicles picking up and delivering young children to and from various schools.

Commentary

1. I was now in business as a raw, untested neophyte with a great deal to learn, largely through trial and error. I profited from mistakes in judgment as I went along.

2. The business world, I found, was far tougher than that of the university – and a world for which nothing I had studied had prepared me. I am embarrassed when I look back on such instances as when I agreed with two insistent friends that they leave their jobs and join me to drive two extra vehicles, thereby adding full-time salaries when the business could support only part-time drivers – an employment arrangement which, fortunately, we established to last only briefly.

3. On the positive side, once I understood the economics of the school transportation business, I was able to enter into firm contracts with the various schools, at fees sufficient to cover all costs and generate a profit. I learned, too, the virtue of not owning the vehicles myself. By using owner-drivers under offsetting contracts to those with the schools, I was able to control costs accurately.

4. It sounds simple, transporting under contract 150-300 children to and from school or camp five days a week, year round. Think, however, about what had to be done to reduce a great deal of complexity to a working simplicity. There were clients to be obtained, licences to acquire, and insurance to arrange. Owner-drivers had to be found, trained and supervised, with vehicles equipped and checked regularly for health and safety, and children to be identified as passengers and pick-ups organized into routes. There was a business style or corporate persona to be established in relation to the qualifications, security, warmth and child-sensitivity of drivers and dispatchers.

   Then, too, in an environment preceding the Internet and the Smart Phone, there were the challenges of getting accustomed to and learning how to use the telephone as the life-line connecting to anxious, easily-ruffled parents; making sure children travelled for only a reasonable time; and gearing pick-up and drop-off times to parent schedules. In addition, invoices had to be prepared and followed up on, cash flow managed, legally-required records kept and taxes paid, and so on.

5. Once the core business was in place and running well, there were expansion possibilities to consider. The challenge of a school bus company, for example, was that vehicles capable of being used more frequently were generating revenue at best only four hours a day.

    It seemed an appropriate next step to expand the school bus company to include a parcel delivery and courier service. Although we could not have compatibly transported raw fish, Chinese food or hot pizza, there were many things we could transport without any adverse effect on our primary business.

    With flexible delivery times for parcels and messages, and our delivery capacity augmented by the use of two scooters, we were able to observe the school bus schedules scrupulously and thereby avoid the dilemmas taxi drivers had experienced.

6. Note the power of need as a driving force in entrepreneurship. In this story, the need which first emerged was no more significant than a personal need to avoid the additional transportation costs that would have been incurred had the school been moved to a new site. This led to a role in school management which, in turn, led to recognition of the school's need for improved transportation. This led in turn, yet again, to recognition of the need for a new transportation system to transport small children.

    I found myself confronting a possible entrepreneurial venture without in any way having deliberately sought it out. Our students needed better transportation. Action was taken to meet it by purchasing a 9-passenger station wagon and having Vinco pick up and deliver 12 children morning and afternoon. This simple action generated a totally-unforeseen response from other schools confronting the same need. Without any sense at the time of what entrepreneurship involved or any previous career aspirations taking me in this direction, I found myself building a new organization. I had become a creative entrepreneur on a small scale.

7. Many more people identify needs than seek to resolve them. Kipling stated the challenge in a different context in "If," his well-known poem: "If you can dream and not make dreams your master; if you can think and not make thoughts your aim." (1895) Although successful entrepreneurs are dreamers and thinkers, what differentiates them, in major part, is their willingness and ability to act in addressing effectively a need they judge sufficiently important to engage their attention. Entrepreneurs travel through dreams and thoughts into action!

8. In this story, we see the interlinkages at work that can exist among entrepreneurial initiatives. A first relatively simple act like putting a single station wagon on the road to transport children can lead to a small school bus company which, in turn, can lead to the complementary expansion into delivery and messenger services.

9. So much of entrepreneurship turns on chance. Had the bank manager not been away when I went to borrow money, I likely would not have been given the loan that was crucial to the growth of the school bus company. At the same time, being willing to seek and take such a loan, and going to the bank armed with a rudimentary business case was entrepreneurial in nature.

10. There are very real benefits from cutting our entrepreneurial teeth on a venture like the school bus company. It was a microcosm of the entrepreneurial world I would later encounter in much greater complexity. The challenges I faced, although a great deal less demanding by comparison, prepared me for the more difficult challenges encountered in subsequent ventures.

11. There is an important "rightness of the times" in relation to entrepreneurship. Some 15 or 20 years later, the business opportunity identified in this case would not have existed.

    First, only in a pre-seatbelt era could we have transported 12 small children in 9-passenger vehicles. Secondly, purely by chance, I had hit upon an existing niche in the transportation sector that needed to be filled – the gap between a taxicab and a regular school bus. I stumbled on this niche by accident but reacted entrepreneurially once I discovered it.

Questions to Consider

1. What primary need was the "entrepreneurial trigger" that set in motion the entrepreneurial initiative, and how was the need identified?

2. Was the resulting action appropriate to meeting the need?

3. As the entrepreneur, did I move into the initiative professionally prepared for the challenges it posed?

4. What impressed you most about the case, positively or negatively, as a learning point for you?

5. The story makes mention, in passing, of obtaining an apartment in the school in return for acting as the school's president. That would not have happened, of course, had there not been some negotiation behind the decision. Can you identify other instances where negotiation was at play in this story? You will see in later stories that win-win negotiating has an important role to play in entrepreneurial success.

Story Five: Glendon Park Nursery School and Day Camp

This story follows immediately on the previous one in terms both of timing and a cause and effect relationship. Had there not been a school bus company, the nursery school and day camp would not have existed. The story moves quickly beyond the challenges confronted in the previous story, however, in illustrating how an entrepreneurial venture can call upon all the strengths the entrepreneur possesses. It also introduces and illustrates the important entrepreneurial factors of "the mind's eye" and "visioning." Negotiation also comes into significant play as a factor in entrepreneurship.

The Story

A year into the school bus operation I was approached by a young couple who were the owners of one of the nursery schools for which we provided transportation. They were trying to determine whether there was a chance our own nursery school might be coming up for sale, as they wanted to move into a larger building with more space for outdoor activity.

Our building was not for sale. Even had it been, however, I had come to believe that, from an educational perspective, it was not the ideal location as it was on a side street off a busy main road. The school, moreover, was in an area of the city that was being occupied increasingly by older parents without young children. I asked the couple, therefore, why they did not look for a more attractive and novel site somewhere within the boundaries of the city but with at least an acre of land, and build a year-round nursery school which would incorporate a special focus on nature and the outdoors.

It turned out they knew of such a property among a number of sites they had been investigating. It consisted of 3½ acres next to the Greenbelt adjacent to a well-populated and relatively new upscale community of young families having children of nursery school age and younger. The site was accessible by school bus from neighboring communities so that, altogether, it sounded ideal. Moreover, the young couple had gone as far as to try to buy the property.

There was a catch, however. Although they had reached agreement on price and made a formal offer to purchase, the owner was insisting on a $20,000 down payment and the maximum they could offer was $10,000. Because the property sounded most attractive, and an eager buyer and willing seller were separated by only $10,000, I volunteered my services as their negotiator.

Our discussion took place on a Sunday morning. While still with the young couple I called the property owner, John Jackson, and arranged to meet him that afternoon at the property. I learned from John and his wife that he had inherited the 3½ acres from the former owner of an adjoining estate of which he had been groundskeeper for many years.

The property was indeed the ideal site for a special type of nursery and primary school. It nestled beside the Greenbelt and seemed far removed from the city while being very much a part of it. I learned also that more than a foot of silt caused by Hurricane Hazel covered the entire property, and construction of new buildings was prohibited.

At one end of the 3½ acres were an old barn in run-down but structurally-sound condition and an unsightly kennel built to house up to 200 dogs. At the other end was the Jackson bungalow. It was this bungalow the young couple intended to re-model to include space for themselves and a nursery school.

The Jacksons were in their late sixties and anxious to put a stressful kennel operation *behind them. Their goal was to move to a bungalow away from the property and build a dog run behind it for several of their favorite dogs. They had estimated, without any serious exploration of possibilities, that they would need $20,000 to cover the down payment on the new bungalow and build the dog runs. They knew, moreover, the general area in which they wanted to live and had verified that it was appropriately zoned.*

This seemed a perfect negotiating situation, especially given that the limited uses to which the property could be put would greatly reduce the number of potential buyers. I asked the Jacksons whether they would sell the property to the young couple at the agreed price but for only a $10,000 down-payment, provided I could help them move to the location they wanted and build their dog-runs for a total up-front investment of $10,000.

When they agreed to this, I took Mr. Jackson to explore the area in which they wanted to live, and to get a sense of what type of home they hoped to buy. We spotted a "for sale" sign on a suitable bungalow – and with dog-runs already in place requiring only minor up-grading.

The next day I contacted the listing agent for the bungalow, verified that the price was acceptable to the Jacksons, arranged for them to see the house and dog-runs, and verified also that the purchase could be arranged for $10,000 down.

The Jacksons liked the new location, were willing to move, and asked me to work with the real estate agent to arrange for the sale of their property for the same $10,000 down. Feeling very good about what had been arranged, I called the young couple and told them everything was all set. They had an ideal property for a special new school, at a down payment they could afford.

At that point everything began to change. The $10,000 for the down payment was to become available only at the end of the nursery school year, six months away. They had to sell their existing house to raise it. It became apparent, moreover, as I pursued possibilities with the young couple, that $10,000 was the most they could hope to realize from the sale of their house. This would have provided no funds for renovations or to transform the site from an unsanitary dog kennel operation into a safe and healthy setting for children.

I had come to believe, however, that the site would be ideal for pre-school education and for a much larger entrepreneurial venture than the young couple had contemplated. In the first place, I judged their choice of the bungalow as their own family home and a school site to be a mistake. Large and attractive though the bungalow was, it had too limited a student capacity once provision was made for their living quarters. Using it, moreover, would be no break from prevailing practice in the field of pre-school education where virtually all existing programs were small ones located in houses of regular family size.

It was the potential of the barn and dog kennels that interested me. I could see both being converted into attractive space for pre-school education. Then, too, in much the way my school bus service was complemented by compatible parcel delivery and courier services, I could see the site also being ideal for a summer day camp, so that the facilities would be in productive use up to 12 months a year and serve a far greater age range during the summer months.

I asked, therefore, for the right to approach the Jacksons on my own behalf, and the young couple agreed this was appropriate. My financial position was significantly worse than theirs, however. I had no capital even locked into an existing property and was not skilled at raising venture capital. Yet I did have regular surplus income from my school bus company. What I worked out, therefore, was one of those win-win arrangements so valuable to entrepreneurs.

The Jacksons wanted to divest themselves of their kennel operation and had no interest whatsoever in the barn, dog kennels or surplus acreage. When I raised the possibility that they continue living in their existing bungalow, they indicated they would be perfectly happy to do so, provided they were free of all property management responsibilities. They wanted and needed, also, the long-term financial security of a regular monthly income equivalent to interest on their equity in the property.

On my part I was young, full of energy, loved small children — Barbara and I having by then both David and his baby sister, Liz — and understood the nursery school business. I had also become convinced the time was right to launch an exciting year-round pre-school program taking advantage of the outdoors.

I was a qualified elementary school teacher with an honour's degree in psychology, a Master's degree with a research focus on the administrative challenges of current child welfare systems, and three years' experience working with children as a social worker. Then, too, through my school bus company, I was in a position to transport students to and from the site from a radius limited only by optimum travelling times.

The proposal I developed, which they accepted, was that the Jacksons would receive a token down payment of $1,000 to bind the property transfer. They would stay in the bungalow, rent-free, for the rest of their lives, and build dog-runs behind the bungalow using materials from the existing dog kennels. In light of their rent-free arrangement I would pay a lesser price for the property than had been agreed to with the young couple and accordingly pay less interest.

To give me time to establish the nursery school and day camp as revenue generators, I would pay no principal for the first two years beyond the initial $1,000 but would be responsible for all the running expenses of the property except their own heat, hydro and telephone. Ownership would be transferred to me but they would register a first mortgage on title.

In turn, I would begin immediately to prepare the dog kennels, barn and grounds for development. These were tasks I could complete without up-front capital, drawing for minor purchases on my school bus revenues. The Jacksons were happy to see them being carried out, moreover, having discovered there was no market for selling the kennels as a going concern. It also helped that they found the idea of having a path-breaking nursery school and day camp on the property an exciting one.

Where my first two entrepreneurial projects had been unquestionably small scale, fitting in well with everything else I was doing, this one was of a different order. At first sight the dog kennels were a most unappealing starting point from which to build what I had in mind. They were filthy, with flies buzzing around in great profusion. The barn was better, being a solid structure which, more obviously than the kennels, seemed capable of being transformed into attractive classrooms and indoor activity areas.

I had in mind that I could burn the midnight oil to complete the first stage of the transformation, and friends and I subsequently did so. Nevertheless, I knew the time would soon come when I would have to find development capital, even though I was not blessed with a great deal of spare time to raise this or to spend on the venture more generally. Although we were no longer living in the nursery school apartment, and I had moved out of my role as the school's President, I still had my family responsibilities, doctoral studies, lecturing, and the school bus company.

Despite the lack of time and capital, I committed to going ahead. It is possible I was at a stage in my life when the university was no longer a satisfying environment. Counting my two years at Teachers College, I had been a student for eight years, with the last six requiring that I take courses each summer as well as during the regular university year in order to graduate earlier.

By another of the chance happenings that help fuel entrepreneurship, some time prior to the Glendon Park initiative I had driven into the university parking lot in one of the bus company's new station wagons. As I was getting out of my wagon, one of my professors drove alongside in a car that was far from new. I waited until he joined me to go into our building and, as we walked along together, he said, "Walter, how is it I'm a professor and you're a student, yet your vehicle is so much better than mine?" My reply was "I'm in business, in a small way," at which point he said that should there ever arise a business opportunity in which he might become involved I should speak to him about it. I remembered this brief conversation when I needed the $1,000 to close the Jackson deal, and took him to see the property.

Fortunately, he had the imagination to see what the transformed property would be like. Standing in the midst of the dog kennels and the flies, I was able to describe it as it would be with seven bustling classrooms of nursery-school children growing in their early development through the quality of the staff, the program, the unique equipment, and the grounds.

At that time, as noted previously, nursery school education was being made available almost exclusively in private homes. I saw real benefits from building-in economies of scale and envisioned seven classrooms of 22 children, with each classroom staffed by two qualified professionals. Staff would have an intimate understanding of childhood development and would help guide children in their growth without resorting to a great deal of creativity-limiting structure.

I visualized each classroom and large outdoor play and activity area having innovative equipment and supplies conducive to pre-school growth, and development programs taking advantage of our special environment. This implied hiring accomplished professionals who, at the same time, were warm and loving people who cared genuinely about children and the individual child.

I visualized, too, the need for busy parents to have their children safely transported to and from school on schedules sensitive to their own needs as well as those of their children. To meet the challenge of the summer months when regular schools close, a complementary summer camp program seemed ideal – and one that could also take older children in addition to those of pre-school age attending year-round. This implied different programming and staffing because a first-rate camp would differ from a first-rate nursery school. A seven-classroom school could accommodate only up to 154 children, moreover, given the restrictions of available classroom space and the licensing requirements covering staff/student ratios. The upper limit of camp enrolment would be much higher, because the camp could use our existing acreage with excursions into the adjacent greenbelt, and summertime structures could be built as home bases to complement the classrooms.

My professor was the first investor, investing initially $1,000. To accept the investment and the rest of the capital we would need, we structured the school as a small business corporation and set about learning the mechanics and legal aspects of raising investment capital. There was legal work, too, in entering into an Agreement of Purchase and Sale with the Jacksons. In such ways I found myself moving into the business world to create "Glendon Park."

Two of my bus drivers were good friends from my home town in England. We worked together into the early morning hours, night after night, stripping away all the unsightly and unsafe wallboard from within the dog kennel building, pulling rusty nails out by the 1,000s, cleaning up after the dogs had left, taking down the large number of dog runs, clearing a planned playground area and, more generally, doing the essential preparatory work for planned construction.

It was a challenge showing prospective parents around the site a month before camp began while we were still in the middle of development. Nevertheless we opened our summer camp with 25 campers, 10 months after acquiring the property.

The Wading Pool

One attractive feature we had in place was an excellent wading pool. We built it from a duck pond we discovered purely by chance. I was walking over the property one day with John Jackson, showing him where we planned to build the nursery school playground in an area roughly 4000 ft. square.

As we approached the far corner, he informed me that somewhere around where we stood was a large duck-pond, buried under silt. He then added, "You know, Walter, it could make a great wading pool for the children. If my memory serves me, it is around 40 foot wide, and even longer than that. It has sloping sides shallow enough that the children could walk down them, and holds about 16 inches of water with plugs and lines for easy drainage."

This sounded interesting. I went immediately to get a shovel and start digging. Sure enough, I hit concrete not far below the surface, and after uncovering a fair piece, found it to be as John had described, with the concrete in good shape. After digging several more test holes, I brought in a Grade-All operator to scrape away the large amount of silt involved, starting from the inner edge of the pool once we found it. It did prove to be 40 feet wide. We kept excavating and uncovered a large area of concrete, all in good condition. I could already envision a wading pool, painted sky blue, with surrounding flagstone, and small children moving merrily in and out of the water.

However, the more concrete we uncovered the closer we came to the wire mesh fence bordering our property. So, over the fence I went with my shovel to determine how far it continued, and discovered some 15 feet of the former duck-pond beyond the fence, on university-owned property. This piece of land was down in the valley away from the university campus and obviously unused, given its overgrown condition. It was scrub land, of no conceivable use to the university but a vital addition in ensuring a new wading pool.

Now, what do you do in such a situation? Do you: (1) ask the Grade-All operator to fill in the area he had uncovered and level the ground; (2) contact the university and seek to purchase or rent the small amount of land involved; (3) build a new waterproof edge within the pool, thereby shortening it by about 10 feet (allowing for the flagstone border); or (4) move the fence? That was not an easy decision. We continued the excavation and moved the fence, rebuilding it to enclose the total additional area we needed for the wading pool and related flagstone.

Some considerable time later, during the second year of the day camp, I invited the university's property manager down to see our new facility. By then it contained the seven-room school within the renovated barn and dog kennels, the nursery playground complete with wading pool, a new shallow swimming pool we had built from "do-it-yourself" plans, and the camp grounds. Everything looked most appealing, with children throughout the whole playground area enjoyably engaged in a range of activities.

When we reached the wading pool, the property manager remarked on how attractive a part of the playground it was. As we stood there, watching the children, his eyes strayed to the fence, and he said, "You know, Walter, I never realized that jog existed in the boundary line – but then, we're never down here!" I told him, then, that we had created the jog, and why. He thought for a moment and then said, "We had better regularize this. I'll draw up a $1 a year lease when I get back to the office." We then went on with the tour.

In the fall we opened the nursery school with 38 children in two classrooms. By the third summer we had a thriving day camp of 300 campers and in the fall a nursery school of 125 students. However, while these were understandably-satisfying achievements, I also experienced the downside of entrepreneurship.

"Origins of Glendon Park: the old barn and dog kennels"

"Glendon Park as it became"

By the beginning of our second year I had completed the coursework for my doctorate. I had also had some success as a lecturer in political studies, working with reluctant engineers in political studies auditorium classes averaging 330 students. Prior to my arrival, teaching these courses had been an unpopular assignment for those departmental faculty who were more research scholars than teachers. For me, it was an enjoyable challenge suited to my teaching background, especially when I obtained approval to substitute multiple choice examination questions for the normal time-consuming essay examinations.

Early in the term I was approached by the head of the department with an offer to join the faculty on condition that I focused strictly on my university work with no outside commitments. I declined the offer, with considerable regret. It would have been impossible to extricate myself from my business activities without Glendon Park collapsing around me.

Had I not been enmeshed in the Glendon Park venture I would have accepted the university position and been launched into a most satisfying educational career. Having to decline the offer caused me to evaluate my overall situation and to realize I had to put my degree and part-time university teaching behind me, temporarily, to focus on the school and camp. I had learned, painfully, that an entrepreneurial venture of any real challenge is a full-time occupation for whatever length of time is required to move the organization beyond its vulnerable start-up stage. I became a full-time entrepreneur on a smaller scale.

By the end of three years, I began to believe my work with Glendon Park was over. We had an excellent staff in place including, together with the teachers, a competent nursery school principal, a strong camp director, an administrative secretary, and a bookkeeper. We had taken shape as a small business and were now ready to move into managerial mode.

Because of the time of year I could not return to university and was, therefore, in somewhat of a dilemma as to what to do next. It happened that my childhood friend Jack, then living in Pontiac, Michigan, had been with his wife Mary and their two children to visit Glendon Park. They had loved what they saw and asked if I would be willing to visit them in Pontiac to assess whether they could and should do on their own three-acre property what we had done on ours. As the next story reveals, this trip led to a new entrepreneurial venture.

Commentary

1. Not everyone who aspires to be a creative entrepreneur should proceed. Inadvertently, I had performed a useful service for the young couple concerning the purchase of the Glendon Park property. They were able to confront their dream squarely with the possibility of making it happen, and to learn something valuable for them to know. They were professional educators and very good at what they did. The husband, moreover, was a rarity in pre-school education at a time when nursery education was almost entirely the preserve of women. They were not creative entrepreneurs, however, who would have experienced special joy from breaking new ground and tackling essential site development before the school and camp could be incorporated. That was fine. We needed professionals in education and it was wise on their part to have shied away from an initiative inappropriate to their real aspirations and strengths.

2. The wading pool situation illustrates an important axiom of entrepreneurship: "Remember it is easier to ask for forgiveness than for permission." The ability to follow this principle without undue stress is one of the differentiators of the entrepreneurial mind. The types of decision involved should not be taken lightly. They could backfire in terms both of cost and goodwill. There are times, however, when seeking permission in advance puts even a sympathetic decision-maker in a difficult position he or she would rather avoid. It is the entrepreneur, therefore, who must make the decision, weighing the factors of integrity, cost, whether what is wanted is sufficiently significant to justify the risk, the departure from form and social conventions, and so on.

    Moving the fence to bring the wading pool fully into the playground was a loose end that needed to be tidied up when the time was right. Despite the element of risk still remaining, it was necessary once the school was operating, with the wading pool clearly a most attractive element, to have the decision authenticated by the university's property manager. Had he not done so, however, we would have clearly needed to consider other less desirable and costly options (e.g., finding a way to keep the wading pool in place totally inside the fence).

3. Managing and the Entrepreneur: After three years, Glendon Park could be move from its entrepreneurial start-up phase into the hands of capable managers. The world of the entrepreneur has much in common with that of the manager. For many years I have been a strong believer in the importance of managing, spreading the word whenever the opportunity arose as teacher and consultant of how vital it is that managerial positions in modern organizations be filled by those capable of managing them professionally.

    Much as I value the role of manager, however, I am convinced that, even among the ranks of high-performing managers, few have the special mind-set, spirit and core attributes required for creative entrepreneurship. If this is indeed the case, that is fine. We need far fewer creative entrepreneurs than we need effective managers.

    Managing is different from entrepreneurship but not less important. Neither is it less demanding, although of a somewhat different knowledge base, skill-set, and orientation. Where creative entrepreneurs add to our stock of existing organizations, or lead especially-challenging organizational growth and revitalization initiatives, managers are vital to ensuring existing and new organizations operate effectively once in place.

    Moreover, competent managers, at every level in an organization and across all functions, recognize and seize opportunities to improve the functioning of their units, generating managerial innovations of value to their organizations. The managerial challenges of settling an organization down and then managing it productively on an ongoing basis are distinctive challenges in their own right.

4. As with managers, leaders are not necessarily creative entrepreneurs, vital though effective leadership is to successful entrepreneurship. One could be a visionary and inspirational leader but incapable of leading the process of creating or transforming an organization when starting out with no more than a preliminary idea.

Because they are so indeterminate, so fraught with risk, and have so many diverse bits and pieces that need to be created and assembled into a coherent yet shifting whole, entrepreneurial ventures require the mind-set, orientation and special competencies of the entrepreneur.

I return later to the special importance of managing and leadership as entrepreneurial attributes and competencies.

5. The Glendon Park story underlines the importance of knowing your strengths and weaknesses. It was driven by the challenges of making my vision real. Once I had achieved that and the project had moved into a managerial phase, I was ready to hand the day-to-day operations over to others with different skill sets.

6. I look back fondly on Glendon Park, both for what it taught me about entrepreneurship and for the joy I experienced from seeing the original vision transformed into such a vital facility.

Through the challenge of building it I learned, for example, how important it is to develop an informed appreciation of the critical importance of money to entrepreneurial success. This is true even when the sector we are involved in is not the business sector. I took like a duck to water in building truly exciting nursery school and summer camp facilities and programs, yet floundered badly at first in relation to finances. I had not realized, for example, how important cash flow was to the survival of the school and day camp. Having no established credit record, new businesses must frequently pay in advance for everything they buy. Even when given short-term credit, they must pay on time from the beginning or lose their credit privileges. New clients, however, may be tardy in paying invoices, unless payment in advance of service is insisted on and such insistence is not a negative factor in acquiring clients.

Cash flows out faster than it flows in. It is a fascinating paradox that a profitable business venture, generating on paper more than it spends, can find its survival threatened on cash flow grounds alone. Then, too, there is the issue of getting optimum leverage from every dollar invested, especially

when investment dollars are in short supply. I was unskilled in such basic matters as developing reliable cost estimates and doing comparison-shopping in
advance of committing to improvements to the property.

Entrepreneurs must move toward decent skill and comfort levels in
handling such financial challenges or they will not survive, unless they have a
special ability to raise capital in excess of their operating needs or are able to
enter into partnership with or hire and use intelligently someone who has the
required financial strengths.

As the Glendon Park story illustrates, entrepreneurs (and their spouses!)
have to be able to tolerate high levels of financial risk and stress.

7. From experience with both Glendon Park and the school bus company, I
developed a new principle of my own, "compatible complementarity", which
subsequently became important in my entrepreneurial career. The school
bus company expanded readily to include a complementary delivery and
messenger service. A day camp was compatible with and complementary to
the nursery school, so that year-round activities were able to make use of the
same property and be integral parts of the overall organization.

8. The story also illustrates the power of visioning as a factor in entrepreneurship. I will return to visioning, but let me draw attention, first, to how strongly the vision in my mind's eye differed from that of the young couple. They
saw and were excited about the possibilities of living in the large and attractive bungalow and converting it into a higher-quality nursery school of the
type to which they were accustomed. To them, the dog kennels were an
unsightly blight on the property which would need to be removed as soon as
possible. To me, the bungalow was inconsequential and hence readily set
aside for the Jacksons, whereas the dog kennels and barn, in conjunction
with the 3½ acres of meadow and the surrounding greenbelt, had exceptional
promise as the ideal site for a special type of nursery school and day camp.
Integrating the day camp into the facility plan as a major part of the total
acreage, moreover, established our credibility as a country facility and supported the year-round programs we had in mind.

Can you see, through this example, what value an entrepreneurial idea and related follow-up insight and vision can contribute to a venture? To both the Jacksons and the young couple, the old barn and the dog kennels were a write-off – a cost factor to be considered in cleaning up the property. To me they were a way to move with little initial capital toward a creative new venture.

9. In relation to Glendon Park I came to realize, again, the critical role the entrepreneur plays during the early years of establishing a new organization. The organization necessarily grows around us simply because of the nature of smaller-scale entrepreneurship. There are very many individual elements that have to be brought together and a complex, interrelated stream of activities that take place. These activities are taking place, moreover, in line with an overall plan that is often nothing more than the somewhat unclear and flexible vision that exists in the mind of the creative entrepreneur. At least during its early stages, everyone engaged in the venture – in whatever role – is either drawn in by or functions around the entrepreneur as the focal point of the evolving organization. The very process of growing the new organization, therefore, places the entrepreneur in a position where too many obligations have been incurred to walk away with an easy conscience.

Questions to Consider

1. What aspects of this story demonstrate that creative entrepreneurship requires of the entrepreneur both an unusually high comfort level with risk and the skill to manage it well?

2. What do you see from the story as being special personal attributes that combine into "the entrepreneurial mind"? How these might differ from the attributes of "the scholarly mind"?

3. Do you find "It is easier to ask for forgiveness than for permission," bothersome? If so, why? If not, why not?

4. In my role as entrepreneur, how important was my academic and experience background to this venture?

5. In what ways was Glendon Park significantly more challenging from an entrepreneurial perspective than the school bus company venture?
6. Can you find examples in this story to support the position that creativity and innovation are vital factors in entrepreneurship?

Story Six: Echo Park

One way to generate wealth in an entrepreneurial way involves first creating a successful small business that lends itself to replication, as McDonald's and other companies have done across the world with their franchising strategies. Such replication, in turn, is simplified because all the systems, processes and practices to assure a successful operation for the first business are in place and might well be readily applicable to similar successor businesses.

As you read the Echo Park story, give some thought to whether, after first building Glendon Park and then an upscale Echo Park in an entirely different community, it would have been feasible to develop a "replicability blueprint" to support building other such parks across Canada and the United States.

The following story introduces several other issues related to entrepreneurial success. The joys, challenges and downside of entrepreneurship are all illustrated. The story also highlights the importance of experience in building the capability to tackle more difficult entrepreneurial ventures and illustrates how a new venture, while raising challenges requiring different strengths, draws on previous entrepreneurial experience at the same time. We begin to see, therefore, the possibility of a career path growing out of a succession of short term entrepreneurial ventures.

The Story

Until compelled to choose between a university career and full-time involvement in an entrepreneurial venture, I had believed I could fit entrepreneurship into my life as a satisfying complement to whatever was then my primary focus. A used bicycle business on campus did not channel much time and energy away from life as a college student. Building a school bus company, parcel delivery and courier service of modest size was somewhat more of a challenge, but still fit reasonably well with life as a graduate student and part-time lecturer. Then, too, in relation to the pre-development phase of building a nursery school and day camp, this was primarily physical labor and that gave balance to my university work.

Moving into the actual development of the school and camp, however, took me into a demanding new phase of entrepreneurial activity and precipitated a choice between two different careers. Yet during the nursery school venture I never accepted that I was embarking on more than a temporary departure from a university career. Even when I made the choice to leave the university, I could already foresee an end to my entrepreneurial career on the horizon.

The visit to Michigan increased the entrepreneurial stakes considerably. It delayed my return to university by a further two years and involved me in a greater entrepreneurial challenge than any I had tackled previously. I became engaged in creative entrepreneurship in a totally unfamiliar community, moreover, and at a time when I had only very limited financial resources to bring to the venture.

I went to Pontiac over the Christmas holidays. Jack and Mary had an attractive home and, as they had told me, it was on a three-acre lot. Yet as I talked over possibilities with them, it became apparent that using the property for a school and camp made little sense, given their professional backgrounds, their location, their lack of anything resembling entrepreneurial activity in the past, and the speed with which the doubts set in when I outlined something of what they would need to accomplish.

They were settled as a family, both working in jobs they enjoyed, and had an active social life. The idea of "building a place like Walter's" stemmed only from how impressed they had been with Glendon Park and the relatively insignificant fact that they had a property of similar size.

Once the decision not to proceed was made, Jack took me out for a drive around the area, including a visit to Bloomfield Hills. Unknowingly, he was leading me toward a new entrepreneurial opportunity.

How do we know that the impulse to move into a new entrepreneurial venture is solidly grounded and not just an irresponsible whim? The answer is that we do not and that it could, in some sense, be whimsical. As Jack was driving me through Bloomfield

Hills – with its magnificent homes set on spacious, beautifully landscaped lots, and its equally magnificent example of a Scottish church, "Kirk in the Hills" – it struck me powerfully as a special place in which to build a private nursery school and day camp, upscale from the one I had built in Toronto but reflecting the same philosophy. When I told this to Jack he dismissed the idea as totally impractical, declaring that so wealthy a community had all the suitable land already tied up in valuable residential real estate. Irrational or not it felt right to me.

Accordingly, I commuted between Toronto and Bloomfield Hills, spending roughly three working days in each. Very early in the process I sought out one of the community's highly-regarded real estate firms, told them of my plans, showed them brochures and a portfolio of photographs of Glendon Park, and requested their help in finding suitable property for a similar enterprise in Bloomfield Hills. I told them, also, that I was not coming with the capital already available. As with Glendon Park, I would be looking to raise the capital locally once I determined there was a suitable site and a sufficiently-sized market.

The real estate company was cooperative. I was given a corner in which to work when in Bloomfield Hills, access to a telephone, and an agent to assist in identifying possible properties. Over time, there proved to be several possibilities, each of which I visited in turn. One came to stand out as being perfect for what I had in mind. Listed for sale as "the Newcomb estate," it consisted of 243 acres in the heart of Bloomfield Hills, on which sat a 26-room mansion.

Decades earlier, the Newcombs had been the leading family in the community, and the house and landscaping reflected this. Yet what had been suited to an earlier era sat uneasily in the new Bloomfield Hills. There was simply no call for such a huge stone mansion when the potential buyers were all wealthy young families of relatively small size. As a development site for residential real estate, moreover, the property had another major drawback—at its lowest point were three small lakes surrounded by ground unsuited to sub-dividing into building lots.

For my purposes, however, the property was ideal. Where those buyers bent on a modern home would be compelled to demolish the mansion at considerable expense, it had a grace and historic charm that made it perfect for a reasonably-sized, economically viable upscale private school for small children, while one of the lakes with its surrounding acreage was ideal as the core of a summer camp site. Accordingly, I asked the real estate agent to set up an appointment with Mr. Newcomb, the executor in charge of the estate, and to let him know I was interested strictly in the house and 36 acres. Coincidentally, as with 68 year-old John Jackson, I found myself dealing with 68 year-old John Newcomb – although there the similarities between them ended.

We met in what had been the palatial living room of the house, the day after I first saw the property. The only furniture was a 10 foot-high grandfather clock, too tall for a modern home but believed to be of significant historic value.

Mr. Newcomb had brought the house plans and a property survey, and we sat on the floor where he spread everything out for me to see. In turn, I had brought the material on Glendon Park. It was a congenial and relaxed meeting. When I told him of my plans he responded by saying his mother had always wanted lots of children on the property and he had toyed, briefly, with the idea of establishing it as a helicopter-accessible camp.

The outcome of the meeting was that I agreed to work towards purchasing the house plus 36 acres for $136,000 US (1960). As part of the purchase agreement, should I proceed with purchasing the house, I would also have a purchase option on a further 56 acres (which we eventually bought), with the acreage to be largely that not suited to real estate development. The terms I proposed for the first 36 acres were a down payment of $15,000 and a first mortgage of $121,000 amortized over 25 years at 6 percent interest. I made it clear I would have to raise the down payment.

One condition of the proposal was that I would pay only $1,000 upon signing (shades of the Glendon Park purchase) and have six months to raise the remaining $14,000, at which time title to the property would be transferred. There was very little negotiation. Mr. Newcomb simply agreed. He agreed, also, that I could move into the house as its caretaker while I raised the $14,000. The real estate agent drew up the Agreement of Purchase and Sale. Jack and Mary loaned me the required $1,000 to close the deal plus a further $500 for living expenses, on the understanding I would find some way to bring them into the project if I succeeded in getting it off the ground. John Newcomb and I signed a Con-ditional Agreement, and I moved into my new temporary home as caretaker.

At the time I had experience only with raising capital from the bank and close acquaintances. I hit, first, on what seemed to be a workable strategy but was very nearly a venture-ending disaster. I knew how much my own family would love the property, being young and outdoors/recreation-oriented, and assumed there must be other young families in the community who would be delighted to collaborate in purchasing the property and developing it as, among other things, our private outdoor recreation area. Accordingly, I designed and had printed a one-page flyer announcing "Echo Park Recreation Club" (the property being located on Echo Road), and distributed this via the local post office to every family in a broad area surrounding the estate.

Two days later I was visited by a grim Reeve, armed with a "cease and desist" order. It turned out that the immediate response to my flyer had been a deluge of calls to his office. The neighbors were up in arms about the project and wanted me out of the neighborhood. For me, having once served briefly as a community recreation director, the term "recreation club" had a warm, friendly, positive ring to it.

To local residents, however, it conjured up the image of bus-loads of drunken teen-agers careening through the neighborhood throwing empty beer bottles out of the bus win-dows. It took me some time to convince the Reeve that this would horrify me as much as it had the neighbors – that what I had in mind was, rather, an attractive variant of a home-and-school club through which young families whose children attended the school and/or camp would join them at the end of the school or camp day and enjoy the facilities together.

After showing the Reeve the material on Glendon Park, convincing him how well it had been received by the community in which it was located, and explaining, also, how positively John Newcomb was supporting the initiative, the Reeve agreed that what I had in mind would, indeed, be suitable for Bloomfield Hills as a new community facility. He said, however, that his hands were tied. Because there was no explicit provision in the zoning bylaw for the planned facility I would need to have two-thirds of the neighbors closest to the estate agree that what I planned was acceptable to them. Accordingly, I went back with him to his office and he gave me a detailed layout of the immediate community, together with a keyed-in list of residents with their telephone numbers.

The closest neighbor was Arnold Braun who, the Reeve had informed me, was a wealthy former businessman who had made his fortune during World War II manufacturing radios for the military. I called Arnold immediately after leaving the

Reeve's office, asked if I could see him and told him why, and he invited me to come the next day for breakfast. Over breakfast I learned that he was only recently retired, beginning to find retirement somewhat empty and, accordingly, was casting about for something interesting to occupy his time. By the end of breakfast – after a host of penetrating questions about my own background, Glendon Park, and what I envisioned for Bloomfield Hills – he gave me his cheque for $10,000.

Much more importantly, Arnold committed to an arrangement of his own devising whereby I would be the bright young builder of a superb primary school (beginning with the nursery school), day camp, and family recreation program, and he would raise the needed capital and lead in ensuring we operated in a businesslike way. By the greatest of good fortune I had found a kindred soul – a creative entrepreneur in his own right, who bought strongly into my vision and had no trouble making up his mind about moving ahead.

Arnold Braun's commitment was an exciting, totally unexpected start to the new initiative. One immediate benefit was that it facilitated greatly getting the approvals I needed for the changes in zoning. This done, I returned to Toronto. I then arranged to have one of the Glendon Park parents who specialized in corporate finance assume the part-time role of Chief Financial Officer, ensured that the Nursery School Principal and the Camp Director were prepared and willing to handle all other aspects of Glendon Park, and began the task of preparing ourselves as a family for the move to Bloomfield Hills.

By then Barbara and I had added our third child Geoffrey to the family, so it was not the simplest of moves. I spent several additional weeks commuting, during which time I prepared the apartment that existed on the second floor of the old mansion, where we were to live. There was some element of déjà vu here. It did not seem too long ago when, as a family of three, we had moved into an apartment above a nursery school. This time – and now as a family of five and with our fourth child, Steven, already on the way – we were to move into a larger apartment above a nursery school that had yet to be built. In reasonably short order we moved to the new apartment, as Canadian visitors rather than permanent residents.

We named the new venture Echo Park, giving it in this way some continuity with Glendon Park. For the first three months I was exceptionally busy with site and program planning, as well as with helping Barbara settle our children into their new schools and the community. There was a business plan to be written which would capture the vision in business-like fashion and include key sections on capital requirements and operating projections, so that Arnold could present the venture intelligently to prospective investors.

In my earlier visits to Bloomfield Hills, I had cleared the way for the property to be suitably zoned for both the school and camp. I had also checked out licensing requirements which proved to be not too different from those in Toronto, and looked in somewhat rudimentary fashion at the marketing aspects of the possible venture, including identifying competitors and verifying prevailing pricing practices. These and other aspects of our plans had to be refined now that it appeared likely we would be proceeding with the project. Meanwhile, in parallel, Arnold was seeking additional investors.

By the end of three months, however, the only investment we had was Arnold's original $10,000, and this was dwindling as we drew on it for living expenses. Arnold was extremely discouraged with the lack of progress. He could not understand why others in the community did not see the prospects the way we did and commit enthusiastically to joining us.

When I looked more closely into what was happening, however, I discovered that Arnold's image as a tough, shrewd, no-nonsense businessman was working against us. Those who knew him well could not accept, coming from him, that the intent was to build a fine community facility and not, as they appeared to suspect, to launch a moneymaking property venture.

How a community perceives the fund-raiser launching a new venture is an important factor. Arnold was respected as a successful businessman and self-made multi-millionaire. He was not seen as someone who could lead in launching a worthy community project. In useful contrast, it helped that I was not perceived to be a businessman but, instead, as someone who had the qualifications and experience to lead the type of venture we had in mind.

I asked Arnold, therefore, for his blessing on my raising the needed capital, pointing out that until we had a secure capital base there was little more I could do to advance program and facilities development and address the challenges of recruiting students, campers and staff. He agreed, with some reluctance, that this made good sense. When I revealed the financing strategy I had in mind, however, he was deeply concerned, believing it was highly unlikely to succeed.

The strategy was a more sophisticated version of the original "Echo Park Recreation Club." We needed $136,000 in equity capital to put us in a strong start-up position. At the same time, we needed a viable strategy for generating solid operating revenue from the day the camp opened. We would also need additional working capital until we reached at least a break-even operating picture.

Accordingly, I proposed that we invite into the project 36 sets of "founding parents," each committing to a $7,500 investment. This amount would be payable over five years. In exchange, and in addition to their ownership shares, each family could participate at no charge in all our activities: the school, the camp, the family recreation program, and a new riding program.

There was a vital "rider" to this investment plan, however. Every founding parent would immediately join us in building the new facilities and, in particular, would be an enthusiastic booster of our programs.

Founding parents, moreover, would have the contacts to attract new parents paying full fees. This was a socially-active community, with couples meeting each other in various places and virtually all of them putting a high value on their children's education and positive leisure activities. With little time remaining to give John Newcomb the rest of his $15,000 down payment, we simply had to move quickly on the investment challenge.

The strategy worked. Where the "recreation club" was a near-disaster, the founding parent strategy was a winner – and in major part because it was so generous to the first investors, especially when they would be joining us to assure the success of a major venture in its earliest stages. The investors, moreover, saw themselves as the founders of an impressive new community facility. This created an atmosphere differing greatly from that created when investors are the founders of a new business venture with expectations of a healthy profit.

Over the next several weeks we were able to find the 36 sets of founding parents. Arnold could never have sold the investment units using this strategy because, on the surface, it was a departure from normal business practice. From the first time people met me, however, they could see I was far more educator than profit-oriented businessman. That I loved children was immediately obvious.

It showed, too, that I knew, intimately, the complementary businesses we planned to be in. I had a vision which, although ambitious, was nevertheless grounded firmly in a realistic understanding of what it would take to pursue it successfully. It helped, also, that they could see from brochures and pictures what we had accomplished with Glendon Park, and that some prudent checking with acquaintances in Toronto revealed that the school and camp did, in fact, exist and were highly regarded.

It was not all plain sailing from that point. When the time to pay John Newcomb the down payment came around we did not have the required $14,000. At a rather dismal meeting Arnold and I had with 8 committed investors a week prior to the payment date the investors were discussing seriously not going ahead with the project. While the discussion was going on, I excused myself temporarily from the meeting, called John Newcomb, gave him an update on our progress, and asked for a six-month extension of the due date. He agreed, readily, and I rejoined the meeting to tell our prospective partners of the new arrangement. Shortly afterwards, John Newcomb confirmed it in writing.

A key part of the strategy was that all investment except Arnold's would be on a contingent basis. No investment commitment would be final until the full $136,000 was committed, at which point a cheque for $700 would be due from each investor to be used for the project. It was reassuring to prospective investors to have this contingency clause in the agreement they signed. It was also the most ethical way to proceed when the venture had a particularly large element of risk.

We closed out the investment very soon after the down payment crisis. The financial standing of the investors, moreover, brought the full $136,000 into the picture when the bank assessed our financial strength and decided on such key matters as the size of our operating line. I had also learned from the Toronto project how important it was to obtain fees in advance for both the school and the camp so that, once we reached the stage where we were ready to accept students and campers, our cash position improved greatly.

The project faced a serious threat, however, as the date for opening our day camp approached. By that point I was fully occupied in developing Echo Park, believing that Glendon Park was in good hands and knowing it had impressive camp enrolment levels. With 300 campers committed we should have been in excellent financial shape, especially as we had moved the previous year to requiring the advance payment of fees.

In financial officer fashion, rather than in the manner a creative entrepreneur might operate, our Chief Financial Officer had paid in full, from the healthy camp revenues, the sizeable debts I had been paying only in piecemeal fashion as we had surplus funds. This meant there were not sufficient funds remaining in the bank account to cover all salaries for the summer staff. Accordingly, a distressed Camp Director wanted my permission to close the camp.

Closing the Glendon Park summer camp would have required the repayment of fees for all 300 campers, thereby precipitating a financial disaster. I explained the circumstances to Arnold Braun, and he agreed to drive with me to Toronto so that we could resolve the situation. He saw as clearly as I did that Echo Park could not succeed unless it received my close attention and that the Toronto challenge, therefore, had to be met quickly.

We did meet it, and in a way that Arnold found most acceptable. Borrowing the funds from him, to be repaid from my Echo Park salary, I deposited summer staff salaries and other camp operating expenses in a special Glendon Park camp account. This enabled us to keep the camp operating throughout the summer until the committed fees had been earned. I then transferred ownership to the able school director and her husband, who very much wanted the ownership position and, together, had the capability to manage the venture year-round.

It was not easy to see my ownership rights disappear. On the other hand, I was now totally free to concentrate on an Echo Park venture that was looking promising. As for the Toronto shareholders, I committed to taking them into Echo Park with me and to giving them a fair share of any ownership rights I acquired.

The visit to Toronto had a positive impact on my relationship with Arnold, in three ways. First, he was able to see first-hand what I had shown him only in photographs and brochures. He was also able to speak with the staff and the children and absorb something of the atmosphere of the program in action. This reinforced strikingly his commitment to our Echo Park plans, and some of what he had learned he passed on to other shareholders and community members in future weeks. Secondly, it gave him a great deal of personal satisfaction that we had saved the Toronto facility through his support, and this offset somewhat his deep disappointment at having been unable to raise the Echo Park invest-ment capital. Finally, and of greatest significance to him, he had seen me sever my contact with what he had viewed from the start as a distraction to what we were building in Bloomfield Hills.

Arnold had wanted my total commitment to Echo Park for years ahead, even though I had made clear to him and every subsequent investor that I intended to return to university once Echo Park was up and running successfully and my role as start-up entrepreneur ended. The investors included powerful business people who, apart from Arnold, saw readily that, if we were as successful as we hoped to be, the time would come when Echo Park would be an established organization needing a different type of person to head it. Although privately-owned, it was to be a local community facility headed by a strong Board of Directors and managed by a competent School Principal and an equally competent Camp Director. Parents would lead the Family Recreation Program while a special committee, overseeing the work of a salaried director, would lead the successful Riding Program.

It was a joy, in the early stages of the venture, to be working with the founding parents on the actual building of the school and camp. Initially, we worked without development capital as there was plenty of preparatory work to be done. The house had been built on the crest of a hill, and the Newcombs had terraced the hillside most attractively. We engaged ourselves in restoring the terraces, weeding them, cutting the rest of the grassy hillside, clearing up the growth on the flat land we wanted as meadows and playing fields, cleaning out the lake around its edges, and opening up riding trails through the bush. What we needed in the loan of farm and gardening equipment was readily forthcoming from enthusiastic founding parents.

Once development capital was available we built our nursery playground which, as in Toronto, was 4,000 feet square. With a retired carpenter who travelled with me from Toronto, we built, first, a pirate ship complete with a crow's nest 5' above the deck, planks to be walked 12 and 15 inches above 'the ocean', and – very attractive to 2½ year old pirates – a large bell to ring (sparingly). In short order, we also built a large sandbox and, starting with a suitably-shallow slope, a tricycle drag-strip circling the sandbox and going under a bridge from which young pedestrians could watch the traffic passing below; a long slide, approached up a railed stairway; a wading pool; a large water-play tub on legs; exciting climbing apparatus – and so on, until we had a safe, stimulating and enjoyable *outdoor play area. We worked, also, to build equally attractive indoor furniture and equipment.*

Supporting what we were doing was a particular philosophy of childhood education. It showed in the fact that, among other equipment, we gave 2 ½ to 5-year-old children supervised access to a vertical 5-foot ladder. When parents came with their young children to determine whether to enroll them in our nursery school, while the parent was talking with me the children would find their way quickly to the pirate ship. When the child was "walking the plank" and jumping down into an imaginary ocean the parent, while watching carefully, would be relaxed. The moment a child found the ladder to the crows' nest, and looked about to climb it, the parent would become anxious and start forward toward her child

At that point I would say, "Hold on for a moment and see what happens" – knowing there was always a member of staff ready to intervene if needed. The child would then almost invariably start to climb the ladder. After the first couple of rungs he or she would look up, look down, look around for Mom or Dad and realize she or he was not coming and very gingerly climb down and move on to another activity. I would then tell the parent that my son Geoff, who was 3 years old at the time, had started up the ladder several times before finally climbing into the crow's nest – and, each time, he had been becoming more capable of climbing it. In this way we built our nursery school around the philosophy that – within reasonable and demonstrably safe bounds – we would structure our equipment and activities around the principle of helping children find comfortable growth possibilities.

The Swimming Pool

To open our summer camp without a swimming pool would have put us at a serious competitive disadvantage. Yet the cost of a pool of the quality required was $25,000 and, therefore, well above anything we could finance from short-term revenue. Accordingly, and in somewhat cavalier fashion considering he had already helped rescue the Toronto facility, I suggested to Arnold that, since $25,000 was a relatively small amount to a multi-millionaire, he might consider loaning it to the project at a fair interest.

Arnold's initial reaction to my request was angrily negative. As he put it, I had arrived in the community without any capital to contribute to the project and received *from him $10,000 in support funding. Yet it was still not clear that the project would succeed – and I had the nerve to ask him to contribute more!*

Coincidentally, however, the investors had agreed some time previously that, on incorporation, I would receive $25,000 in ownership shares for my contribution to the project. Accordingly, I told him that if he would put another $25,000 at risk I would match it with my $25,000 in shares, by agreeing in writing that I would be entitled to the $25,000 only if the Board of Directors agreed, at the end of the second year of operation, that the project was an unqualified success. Arnold agreed, and we built our new swimming pool.

I will address, later, the need on the part of the creative entrepreneur for a balanced reverence for money – that is, to value it but not excessively. In this case it shows in my willingness to ask Arnold Braun to finance the swimming pool – believing genuinely that $25,000 to a multi-millionaire was relatively very little – and, at the same time, being willing to give up the certainty of a $25,000 ownership position in recognition that, to Arnold, there needed to be an offsetting benefit if his business sense was to be satisfied.

I had seen the Newcomb property early in January. By July 1ˢᵗ of that year we opened our summer camp with 75 campers, and opened our nursery school in the fall. By the second summer we had 200 campers, and at the end of the summer were rated #2 in day camps in Michigan. The nursery school opened its second year with 88 students so that, altogether, what we had envisioned was coming together very well.

By any reasonable standard we were firmly on course to becoming a successful business. As well, we had created a most attractive community facility consisting of a nursery school, a day camp, a family recreation program, and riding stables. The 92 acres we owned by then were in productive use seven days a week, year-round, through the effective blending of complementary and compatible activities serving children and families.

When the time arrived to decide whether I had earned the $25,000 in shares I had voluntarily surrendered, earlier, the Board Chairman asked me to leave the Board Meeting briefly, so that the assessment of my performance could be made without my being present. By this time we had a strong Board of Directors, members of which were Chairs or Board Members in other corporations and familiar, therefore, with how boards were meant to work. A fact of some significance was that, over the previous two years, the *composition of the Board had changed in the number of new members it contained who were unfamiliar with the impressive start-up and growth of the facility.*

The Chairman called me back into the meeting to tell me that the Board had concluded that I had accomplished everything I had promised and had voted unanimously to confirm my ownership of $25,000 in shares. The Chairman then went on to tell me, however, that they had also concluded – again unanimously – that it was vital to the school and camp that I provide the required leadership for the next five years. Accordingly, they had decided to follow a practice that was standard with major American corporations, and that was to assign me the shares I had earned over five years, at the rate of $5,000 a year.

This was a group I had brought together. They had accepted my leadership without question for two years and, together, we had brought into reality a complex, truly challenging vision. Because I had never hidden my intention to return to university, and my agreement to surrender my $25,000 contained no clause for sequential payment over five years, I saw their decision as an act of bad faith.

I rejected their offer shortly after the Board Meeting, and told Board members that unless they lived up to the original commitment I would vacate my position at the earliest time I could prepare the staff to function without me. This was not a bargaining ploy on my part. The very fact that the Board had decided as they did broke the vital links an entrepreneur establishes and I knew it might well be time to leave. An important consideration in my own decision-making had remained the strength of my desire to return to university, and the Board was undoubtedly concerned about this.

Our first site of the of the
soon to be Echo Park

Echo Park in Action

Crow's nest in play
structure

Leaving Echo Park

The decision to leave Echo Park was difficult for the Board to understand. Individual Board Members told me, over the next several days, that I should see their decision as a strong vote of confidence in my leadership, and accept graciously that what they had proposed was sound business practice to retain key employees. I never saw myself as "a key employee." I was a creative entrepreneur at my best as a builder. I had no interest in transforming myself into the Executive Director of a small organization, even one I had played a leading role in creating.

At the end of the month we left Echo Park, without the $25,000 in shares and with only a month's pay in hand. By this time, we had five children. Our son Steven and daughter Mary had been born during the two years we were in Bloomfield Hills.

The months immediately after leaving Echo Park were bleak. During the next six months, I first worked unsuccessfully as a social worker, after which we all moved to live with Barbara's Mom, Reta, while I worked in the local liquor store at minimum wage. We were fortunate that Reta welcomed us warmly as temporary visitors and our children all found the schools they needed.

Three months later, I returned to university.

To move beyond Echo Park I needed a major challenge on which to re-focus my energies. Returning to university to begin a second doctoral program was such a challenge, made more so because I had no funds on hand to ensure I would be able to support Barbara and five growing children while at university.

Rather than going back to Toronto, I applied and was accepted at Queen's University. Enrolling once again at Queen's was like returning home. Most of my former graduate school professors were still there and accepted me as if there had been only a brief hiatus since completing my Master's degree.

Upon acceptance I was given a $2,000 graduate fellowship. In short order I was able to line up appointments as a part-time lecturer in political studies, at both Queen's and the Royal Military College. I taught also at Queen's summer school during the first and second summers and acted as its Executive Director for the third summer. I acted, also, after the first year, as Executive Secretary of the Department of Political Studies so that, *altogether, we managed well financially throughout the compulsory minimum three years required to obtain a doctorate.*

Commentary

1. The incident with the Reeve underscores the importance of developing an understanding of the local culture in which we plan to work, in advance of settling on a financing strategy. Had I been wiser in the ways of entrepreneurship I would perhaps have tested the recreation club strategy in advance with local residents.

2. Yet the incident also underscores the importance of being able to think fast on one's feet. Had I not moved the perception of the Reeve concerning what I hoped to initiate from that of a most undesirable recreation club to an attractive community facility, I would never have gained his cooperation in identifying local residents. There are times like this, when on occasion we are able to turn what appears to be a serious problem into a valuable opportunity.

3. As entrepreneurs, we should never underestimate the importance of the likeability factor and, related to this, the ability to work well with people who differ from us in significant ways. In rapid succession, and as someone without capital to contribute, I had to deal with a well-established real estate firm, the wealthy owner of the Echo Park acreage and mansion, the Reeve in his official role, Arnold as a retired and tough businessman, Arnold's gracious wife who had joined us for breakfast, and later, each prospective Founding Parent. Had we not liked each other, sensed some measure of compatibility, and developed a comfort level in relation to integrity and ability, the venture would have gone nowhere.

    To be of value, the entrepreneur's likeability factor cannot be, or be seen to be, glib salesmanship. It has to be much deeper and more solidly based than this, stemming from a number of interrelated, more basic factors. We will build the relationships so essential to creative entrepreneurship if we approach other people readily and are comfortable being with them; if we are open in our relationships and sensitive to differences; and if we tend to be happy, optimistic, with a strong joie de vivre. We need to be active, empathetic listeners while communicating clearly whatever we want to communicate or our listeners want or need to hear. We must genuinely be interested in people as individuals, have a strong commitment to whatever interests us at the time and be sincere in wanting the views of others.

4.   In complement to the likeability factor, it was also important that I had taken steps to be prepared – with an intriguing vision, certainly, but also with photographs and brochures from Glendon Park. It was also important that I had carried out enough local research to be able to address issues of market niche, competition, and pricing.

5.   It is the combination of likeability, perceived integrity, vision, relevant background and capabilities, and some evidence of solid if preliminary research that comes together to generate the required level of trust. I was asking John Newcomb to commit the required real estate for a $1,000 token payment and to let me move onto the property as interim caretaker. The Reeve had to trust me enough to release names and telephone numbers and give me his support. Most importantly, Arnold had to accept me as a young colleague he could trust with a cheque for $10,000 to be used for personal support, and as the person whose vision and trustworthiness he would sell to the community.

None of this can be faked. We have to be someone the people we need to work with can trust and relate to positively. After all, we are putting ourselves forward as leaders, asking others to join us in initiatives which, by their nature, we will need to control as entrepreneurs.

6.   We tend to regard an agreement as final simply because it has been signed by the parties to it. It is not "final," however, if the parties later agree it should be changed. It was perfectly appropriate for me to go to John Newcomb for an extension of the time to allow us to raise the down payment. It was, after all, advantageous to him to keep the venture alive. Once we do sign an agreement, however, we are likely to become committed to its successful completion even if this requires that it be modified.

7.   The story illustrates the importance of passionate commitment in ener-

gizing the creative entrepreneur. Until the Board decided to issue my shares over a five-year period, I had radiated the forward drive, energy, commitment, enthusiasm and excitement required of the entrepreneur in a complex start-up venture – all of which was generated by a deep attachment to the initiative. Literally overnight that attachment disappeared, permanently.

I was so fully committed and focused that I was changing the basic nature of what we actually produced and how we managed our business affairs. Echo Park, after two years, was a solidly grounded community facility under the leadership of a strong Board of Directors with the required supporting staff.

8.   There is always the possibility that a creative entrepreneur will put his or her family at risk. That I did so in relation to Echo Park was one of the most difficult parts of the decision to leave. Immediately after the Board Meeting, Barbara and I discussed leaving. We agreed it was time to do so. It was up to me at the time to ensure that the decision would not harm our family. Yet I knew such harm was a distinct possibility. Leaving a secure position, without another one to move to cannot help but put a family in jeopardy, especially if there are no financial reserves on which to draw.

I look back on Echo Park as a special period during which I was engaged mind, heart and soul in leading the building of something of which we could all be justifiably proud. Yet I remember the several months following our departure from Bloomfield Hills as the most painful period of our lives. I was psychologically bruised by what I experienced as rejection by colleagues. Without a job, and with my sense of self-worth at a low point, I had to find a way to support our family of seven.

My friend Jack, who by that time was active in Echo Park and a member of the Board, could not understand even remotely how I would put my family at risk by moving out of a situation in which I had a decent salary, a nice apartment, $25,000 assured to me in share-holdings, parents and staff who truly appreciated my work, and students and campers I enjoyed being with immensely.

9. It is the total nature of the commitment that leaves the entrepreneur vulnerable to the pain of a major setback. One can truly care too much. As I noted earlier, the challenge is to enter every entrepreneurial project knowing that, by its very nature, it is fraught with risk and might well not succeed. We need to be prepared to move on from the venture without allowing it to be self-destructive.

    That the Board denied me immediate possession of my ownership shares was, in retrospect, nowhere near as reprehensible an act as I saw it at the time. It was simply an example of the "Eye of the Beholder" phenomenon. Through their eyes, Board Members were behaving supportively and prudently in the interests of the long-term success of a fine community facility, and were giving my leadership a strong vote of confidence. Through my eyes, it was a betrayal of trust and commitment. I knew that because I did see their decision in this way, my value to the venture was finished. Thinking back on the situation, I realize I had something to learn about managing a Board of Directors.

10. Faulty communication was also a factor. Each of us communicates from within our own unique psychological life-spaces. We interpret what we hear on the basis of who we are. Consequently, we will sometimes hear what we want to hear rather than what someone else is trying to tell us. I was convinced I had communicated clearly that I intended to go back to university as soon as the entrepreneurial phase of our venture was completed. Yet the Board of Directors believed I would stay for a further five years rather than give up $25,000 in shareholdings.

    The issue was, in major part, a question of timing. There is no doubt in my mind that, towards the end of my involvement, I was close to being redundant. We had excellent permanent staff in place, a solid clientele, proven programs, community acceptance and support, and a strong Board of Directors. In my judgment, there was no longer any need for my involvement and the time was right to begin working towards re-admittance to university.

As I outline in Chapter Three, leaving Echo Park, though so painful at the time, turned out to have been the right career decision.

Questions to Consider

1. Drawing on this story, how critical is passionate commitment to entrepreneurial success?

2. Can you see how and why likeability is so important in entrepreneurship, and how it relates to preparation and trustworthiness?

3. What strategic considerations influenced the choice of a financing strategy?

4. Why, as entrepreneurs, should we treat written agreements as open to renegotiation no matter how "final" they are? At the same time, when would a written agreement have been especially helpful in this venture?

5. What is the "Eye of the Beholder" phenomenon, and how was it important in relation to Echo Park?

6. In what ways does being "a creative entrepreneur" differ from being "a key employee"?

CHAPTER THREE
Intrapreneurship-in-Action

Although similar in many respects, the role of intrapreneurs or *intra-corporate* entrepreneurs (Pinchot 1985) differs from that of entrepreneurs because they practise entrepreneurship inside existing organizations which benefit from their efforts. While entrepreneurs have the treasured freedom to pursue their own visions, unconstrained by more senior levels of an organization or colleagues' expectations, that freedom is offset considerably by a lack of supports that may be available when working inside an established organization.

Intrapreneurs are committed to supporting the organization's growth, revitalization and/or reorganization in some significant way and obtain special support from being part of the existing organization. However, there is a cost as well. In exchange, they must work within and be sensitive to the organization's traditions and constraints, and be guided by strategic directions established by more senior decision-makers.

The stories that follow describe three ventures in intrapreneurship. The first takes place within the Faculty of Administrative Studies at York University. Anyone familiar with both university and business environments will know how they differ from one another. The second venture occurs in the complex environment of the Canadian federal Department of Public Works which, although involved closely with the business sector in its design and construction activities and project delivery, functioned differently from organizations in the business sector. The third focuses on the design and delivery of an international conference under the auspices of the Canadian Association for Future Studies (CAFS).

As you read each story, be alert to the similarities and differences between the intrapreneurship they illustrate and entrepreneurship that was the focus of the stories in the previous chapter. These are addressed at the end of each story under the commentary.

Story Seven: Building a School of Public Policy and Management

Universities differ markedly from business organizations in the types of organizational cultures they create. The dominant activities of members of the Faculty are academic research, writing and teaching. The primary professional strengths considered in recruiting and appointing staff are the possession of a PhD or equivalent in some relevant field of study, the strength of a continuing commitment to academic research and writing, and the commitment and ability to function effectively in an educational capacity.

Although there is necessarily provision within a Faculty for managing its affairs, this is not so much esteemed as tolerated in a largely anti-bureaucratic environment. Yet requirements do exist to create and function within clearly defined operating units such as faculties, schools, departments and the like. It is a challenge to bring a new entity into being and, in doing so, to work sensitively within the values, traditional ways of doing things, and existing power structures within which the decision-making processes functioned.

The Story

After graduating with a doctorate from Queen's, I was offered and accepted a position at York University as an Associate Professor. This led, shortly after my arrival, to taking on responsibility for building a new School of Public Policy and Management. For the first time, I was able to fit creative entrepreneurship into my university career.

I joined the Faculty of Administrative Studies at York. This was a faculty in name only and functioned at the time as a School of Business, with involvement also with

Hospital Administration. Keenly aware of this, the Dean wanted to enrich the Faculty by adding a School of Public Administration. Students entering the Faculty could then prepare for careers in the public, business or health sector, and professors could support all sectors through their research, publications, teaching and consulting.

When I joined the Faculty, there were 80 faculty members of the School of Business. There was also a lone faculty member whose work was directly in the field of public administration. Two years prior to my arrival, he had accepted with reluctance the task of building a School of Public Administration but had found it difficult to move the project ahead in a faculty so oriented toward business. I became the second public administration faculty member and, very soon after my arrival, was asked by the Dean to take on responsibility for building the new school.

While at Queen's I had become convinced that "public administration" was not an appropriate name for my specialty, believing that the more appropriate one would be "Public Policy and Management". This was not a minor quibble over semantics. The discipline had arisen within political studies and hence had a major interest in the political system, in general, and public policy processes in particular.

Given the importance of managers to be productive in public sector departments and agencies, there needed to be an equally-strong concern with how well policy development is supported and translated into action by public service managers and public policy specialists. While a good friend and colleague at Queen's was busy launching a new School of Public Policy with close ties to its Political Studies Department, I foresaw building a School of Public Policy and Management as part of the Faculty of Administrative Studies with close ties to the School of Business and only a somewhat distant relationship with York's Department of Political Science. When the Dean asked me to build the new school, however, I asked that he let me first build a School of Social Policy and Management.

As its name indicates, this would have focused on the social services sector rather than the public sector. Work with the Kingston Children's Aid Society while an undergraduate student had led to my continuing interest in child welfare, and my Masters and PhD research had been in this field. I had taken the necessary courses at St. John's College to qualify for work as a teacher with juvenile delinquents and had come to Canada or-iginally with the hope of working at Shawbridge Boys' Farm in Quebec, a highly regarded school for juvenile delinquents. I had worked, too, as a teacher with poverty-stricken Ojibwa and French-Canadian children. For many years, therefore, I had had a strong interest in the social services sector.

Experience with the sector had convinced me that managers in social service organizations had the same need for professional education in policy and management as those in the business and public sectors. A Faculty of Administrative Studies seemed the proper place for policy and management studies in relation to all three sectors, with students being educated together in policy and management fundamentals while at the same time preparing themselves in their respective schools to work in their chosen sectors.

Within the public sector there was evidence of an emerging interest in the challenges of preparing managers more effectively. This interest had been strengthened considerably through the work of a Royal Commission on Government Organization which raised the profile of managing as a key public service role. In the social services sector, however, the profession of social work itself was still in its infancy and the existing university schools of social work were focused on graduating competent social work practitioners.

For practical reasons having to do with the size of the foreseeable market and the availability of potential funding support, the Dean remained firm in his decision to move first on a school for the public sector. He committed, however, to supporting the development of a School of Social Policy and Management immediately following the establishment of the public sector school, acknowledging that with schools focusing on four sectors (incorporating Hospital Administration as the fourth sector), the Faculty would become a richer and more diversified Faculty of Administrative Studies. I agreed to build what he wanted, but requested and was given the right to identify the school as a School of Public Policy and Management.

I arrived at the Faculty in late June, shortly after completing my doctorate. The Dean's advice was to take the summer off except for preparing my fall classes. He did not foresee opening the new School until a year from the coming fall and assumed a full year of advance preparation would be more than adequate. Much as I would have enjoyed a summer vacation, however, the Dean's assumption appeared sufficiently critical to require careful testing.

Envisioning a School of Public Policy and Management as it would be, once in place, I traced in my mind the steps that would need to be taken. They struck me, even on cursory review, as constituting a formidable challenge not easily met within 12 months. I then cast around for someone with an intimate knowledge of the university's decision processes and approval requirements and found this in the person of York's Corporate Secretary.

The Secretary was able to show me that to gain approval for a new school would involve crossing 14 decision hurdles in sequence, each involving a separate decision body. Even with careful preparation and ongoing diligence, it would still be touch-and-go to obtain the required decisions within a year. He told me that there would also need to be a fully-developed proposal, approved in advance by our own Faculty, before we could enter the University approvals process. The approval would be needed by early in September or the opening of the new school would be delayed by a full year.

Learning this brought home in a forceful way that I was moving into a new role as intrapreneur rather than entrepreneur. I had been only a creative entrepreneur to this point, building small business organizations to pursue original visions. The leadership of each venture had largely been in my own hands as entrepreneur. To perform as an intrapreneur, I needed to come to terms with the organizational environments within which I would now have to work.

Although familiar with a university environment in general, I was not familiar with York University as the setting in which the new school was to be situated. In the first place, I had the Dean to work with and, although I could and did influence in a minor way the direction in which he wanted to take the school, he was the Faculty's acknowledged leader in setting strategic directions. In turn, he had the members of the Faculty to influence, virtually all of whom possessed PhDs. which signified proven expertise in their particular specialties, and each looked to the Dean to support his or her specialist goals and aspirations. In a manner that would surprise executives from the business sector, a university dean faced with an important Faculty decision must engage in discussions with faculty about whatever strategic position he wants the Faculty to take. If he fails to win faculty members over to his position, he may not be able to move ahead. In relation to the evolving School of Public Policy and Management in particular, there were several environments important to our decision-making.

Although the internal environments of the School of Business and the School of Public Policy and Management would both have important roles to play, each would exist within the environment of the Faculty of Administrative Studies. The Faculty, however, was one part only of York University, and the Faculty and University could both exert decision constraints on plans to build the new school.

There were also constraints on the University itself. Its external environments included Ontario's university system which contained a number of Canadian universities and colleges, and the Province of Ontario which provided significant funding.

With respect to our internal decision-making, we had to fit the Faculty effectively into the broader university environment and be sensitive to university requirements and expectations. We also had to be careful that the proposed new directions were targeted toward healthy markets to ensure that there would be an active demand for the services of our graduates. There were also funding authorities with their particular interests to consider and other faculties competing for whatever share of available resources they could negotiate in the challenging budget processes of the University. Then, too, the existing School of Business had its own special axe to grind within the Faculty.

Somewhere in all of this was the blossoming idea that a new School of Public Policy and Management would be a good fit within a Faculty of Administrative Studies alongside the School of Business.

Without the Dean as its champion, we could not have moved the new school forward. But without a committed creative intrapreneur acting on his behalf, the Dean's wish to have a new school had remained unfulfilled. Moreover, unless the Dean had the faculty behind him, we could not move ahead with the school. Even with the Dean's support and the blessing of faculty, the new school had to conform to the general requirements of the university along some key dimensions.

To lead in building a new School of Public Policy and Management, we had to learn where the power to support or impede such building lay, what the decision processes and their time-lines were, what particular form proposals should take, and so on, to come to grips effectively with what was to me a largely unfamiliar decision environment.

There was also the factor of my own perception of what should result from all of this, captured in a vision of the end state toward which we should be working. I envisioned a

School of Public Policy and Management working in close harmony with the School of Business and later, also, with a School of Social Policy and Management. To keep the School relevant to the environments it would serve, I saw it having a strong Advisory Board composed of top managers from federal, provincial and municipal public services. I saw, too, the student body being drawn to some important extent from current and prospective managers already working in one of the public services.

It was consistent with this vision for the school that the number of new faculty having a specialty in public policy and management could be limited to significantly fewer than those staffing the School of Business. This was feasible because the so-called "business" specialties applied equally to all four of business, public, health, and social service sectors and, with only minor restructuring of individual courses, separate programs could be developed for the different schools. We would look to specialized clusters of faculty, such as a cluster in Organizational Behavior, to ensure they were staffed with those able to work effectively with students from the different schools.

Consistent with the vision, too, we recruited the members we needed for the planned Advisory Board over the summer. What brought members willingly to the Board was, in major part, their belief that what we planned to put in place merited their support. They shared the belief that we needed to equip public sector managers with the best of business sector knowledge and skills while also strengthening their understanding of, respect for, professional commitment to, and ability to work effectively within the public sector.

They also liked the planned professional orientation of the School. Although it was to be committed to high academic standards, its primary professional role would be to develop public sector managers and their policy and management support specialists, and its research and consulting would be focused on improving organizational performance.

Creating the Advisory Board was an important step. It gave the new school credibility in the markets we planned to serve and from which we intended to draw students. The 25-member Board consisted of 16 of the Government of Canada's top deputy ministers, 6 top deputy ministers from the Province of Ontario, and 3 Chief Administrative Officers from leading municipal governments.

Building the Board over the summer was not a simple matter. Members had to be recruited through at least one face-to-face meeting with each, and persuaded in such meetings of the worthwhile nature of the initiative and of why they should commit their considerable prestige and scarce time to helping make it a success.

Although not my own highest personal priority, the planned new School did engage me strongly. I had developed at Queen's into an advocate for the vital contribution effective managers make to an organization's well-being. I had also come to believe that business, government and the not-for-profit sectors all needed a new breed of manager equipped to function at a significantly-improved professional level, and saw York's management faculty playing a strong role in the preparation of such managers in two key ways. First, there was a generic core of knowledge, skills and values needed by managers regardless of the sector in which they planned to work. Secondly, managers needed to understand their own sectors very well but to understand other sectors, also, given the complex inter-relationships that exist across sector boundaries. A management faculty serving major sectors would be a natural place to acquire such understanding.

The required proposal was ready for review and approval by faculty by September, in the form required to enter the university's lengthy approvals process. Close interaction with the Dean and certain influential faculty who happened to be around during the summer had produced a proposal that took account of Faculty decision realities and was one the Dean could champion strongly. Given his understanding of the University's decision pro-cesses, the Dean was able to ensure that the proposal was properly sensitive to these. As a consequence, with some hiccups along the way, the proposal received Faculty and Univer-sity approval within the twelve months scheduled for approval purposes. This cleared the way for the considerable work required to activate the School.

Once we had approval for this, we had to bring a new school into existence over a short time span. There was a curriculum to design; a school calendar, brochure and other marketing pieces to prepare; and admission procedures to establish. Students had to be recruited and processed, faculty hired, library holdings to check and augment. Study schedules had to be set, classroom and seminar rooms arranged, and so on. We opened on schedule. I was the School's first director while, at the same time, being active in my role as an Associate Professor.

Managerial skills proved once again to be essential to intrapreneurial success. It was one thing to develop an exciting vision, convert this into a detailed decision-ready proposal, and manage the proposal through a complex decision process. It was quite a different set of challenges to actually set up the school, especially as the decision process itself had taken up much of the year preceding its planned opening.

The required planning and approvals processes could not take place in advance of implementation action in some neatly sequenced way. A less entrepreneurial approach might have been to reserve a year for approvals and the following year for start-up activities. Instead, we moved as far and as fast as we could on implementation, in parallel and intertwined with the approvals process.

The decisions we need and the supporting plans we develop as precursors to getting an initiative like this off and running are at somewhat of a broad-brush level. Flowing from them and not requiring the same level or breadth of approval are the more detailed plans and procedures required for implementation. Within the entrepreneurial process, we find ourselves involved in each of the detailed responsibilities central to a manager's job. All of these activities must take place under the pressures of tight deadlines, and within pre-existing organizational expectations and ways of behaving with which we must conform in major part.

As we neared the end of the school's second year, the time seemed right to begin work on the School of Social Policy and Management. With the Dean's blessing, I took forward a proposal to this effect to Faculty Council, in the expectation it would be endorsed strongly as the logical next step in expanding the Faculty.

As faculty debated the proposal, however, it became apparent it was not going to be endorsed. After seeing the School of Public Policy and Management emerge alongside the School of Business, a predominantly business faculty may have become uncomfortable with the move away from their own primary focus on the business sector. It is possible they were not yet really at ease with the concept of a Faculty composed of equally powerful schools, working from a common generic base but each with its distinctive sector focus.

When it became clear the time was not right to launch the second new school, the Dean offered me the opportunity to take a year's leave of absence to work within the federal public service on social policy issues. In making the offer, he held out the possibility of re-introducing the School of Social Policy and Management proposal on my return, when the decision climate of the Faculty might well have changed. I accepted his offer, and went to

Ottawa to meet with John MacDonald, the Deputy Minister of Indian Affairs and Northern Development and a member of the School of Public Policy and Management's Advisory Board, to explore possibilities of spending my year in Ottawa as a temporary member of his policy staff. This, in turn, led to new intrapreneurial activities within the federal government.

Commentary

1. New insights can be instrumental in the recognition of an entrepreneurial opportunity. There are several such insights at play in this story. They include the reorientation from "public administration" to "public policy and management"; the consequent shift in orientation from seeking a kinship with political studies toward a kinship with policy and management studies; and a recognition that the social services sector had as strong a need as other sectors for professionals skilled in policy development and analysis and in managing.

    How we name a venture can be an important consideration. To keep the new school separate from the Department of Political Studies, it made good sense to use a name establishing its role more clearly within a faculty housing a school of business and with a vested interest in public policy and management.

2. The Dean's request that I build the new school illustrates an important aspect of entrepreneurship – namely, that we do not always have to search for entrepreneurial opportunities. Sometimes they are offered to us when someone, other than ourselves, identifies a need for entrepreneurial strengths and concludes we just might have them to the level required.

3. The story shows also that entrepreneurs, whether creating new organizations or working as intrapreneurs within existing organizations, have the tendency to want to shape such opportunities when offered, either to make them better suited to their own interests and strengths or to make them more interesting and exciting. There is always the danger, however, of killing one opportunity in pursuit of a second, more exciting one. This was the situation

when I sought approval for a School of Social Policy and Management rather than immediately supporting the Dean's desire to have me build a School of Public Administration. Fortunately, I did not exceed the Dean's tolerance for contrary ideas.

4. Intrapreneurs frequently work within layers of interlocking environments and need, therefore, to develop a sense of the layering and intermingling of their environments. They also have to develop the ability to factor this understanding into their decision-making.

5. Within the broader concept of the environment there is the important factor of culture. The culture of a university is not that of a business organization. Certain fundamental values and ways of operating are different and we need to understand this if we are to work effectively in the particular culture.

6. Both entrepreneurs and intrapreneurs are storytellers. Recall, in particular, the process of building an Advisory Board around individual meetings with top public servants. I had to have "the story" ready and tell it consistently and persuasively, both within the Faculty initially and then in each of the relevant University decision committees.

7. In the kind of decision environment within which I had to work, it was not only essential to have a clear vision of the end state toward which we were working, but to be persuasive in ensuring that business-oriented faculty did not threaten where we were heading.

8. As creative entrepreneurs some of our best, most exciting and potentially most fulfilling visions may never be realized. I look back on my experience at York with considerable regret. Had I been able to launch the planned School of Social Policy and Management, it would have been my most fulfilling venture and have occupied me for the rest of my working life.

In retrospect, because I did not anticipate any serious difficulty in moving forward with the School of Social Policy and Management as expeditiously as we had moved on the public service sector school, it was a serious mistake not to have prepared individual faculty for approving the proposal before I took it to Faculty Council for decision.

There are two key aspects of ensuring that proposals are "decision-ready"; namely, preparing a professional proposal, and working in advance of taking it forward for decision to ensure a receptive decision-making body. It was this second aspect I neglected.

9. In the course of building the School of Public Policy and Management, I experienced some similarities and differences between functioning as an entrepreneur and then as an intrapreneur. The most fundamental similarity between the two is that there is a common need in both for an entrepreneurial mind, spirit and core competencies. What I had experienced as an entrepreneur was not dissimilar in microcosm to what I came to experience as an intrapreneur, even though I was practising my intrapreneurial role in a much larger and more complex organizational environment.

Like entrepreneurship, intrapreneurship is an art because of the essential creativity underlying it. The artistic medium in which we work as intrapreneurs consists of the same materials of which organizations are constructed in the first place by entrepreneurs and can be employed, therefore, in an organization's reconstruction. As with entrepreneurship it is also a craft, in that it rests on acquired knowledge and skills honed over time through experience. The longer we remain active as intrapreneurs, the more committed we are to continuous learning, and the more professionally we come to perform the role.

The story reveals another similarity. Intrapreneurial activity takes place in other sectors of society as well as in the business sector. Many of those who write about intrapreneurship focus on the business sector, because of its productivity potential or its importance for sheer survival in turbulent economies. Yet there are also intrapreneurs applying their strengths fruitfully in the public and not-for-profit sectors.

10. There is a regular need to adapt, reorient and renew public organizations at every level of government. Governments face their own particular pressures from turbulent environments, and public policies change regularly and sometimes fundamentally, depending on which political party is in power and

individual occupants of political and executive roles. Policy changes and key initiatives launched at the highest levels of the public service lead to an equally constant need to reorganize and revitalize public organizations and their internal processes, practices and systems. This is true, also, of the not-for-profit sector which constitutes so large a part of modern developed societies.

Questions to Consider

1. What do you see as the key similarities and differences between functioning as an entrepreneur and as an intrapreneur? Which of the two roles seems to fit you better, and why?

2. What differences in culture exist between the university and business sector environments?

3. Why was "tough-mindedness" an important intrapreneurial attribute in this case?

4. Did the time it took to assemble the School's Advisory Board surprise you? To what particular entrepreneurial attributes was the time factor related?

5. Given the similarities between entrepreneurship and intrapreneurship, is it reasonable to expect that someone of entrepreneurial mind, spirit and core competencies could succeed equally well in both if strongly motivated to do so?

6. A key factor in intrapreneurial success is to first identify a suitable intrapreneurial opportunity to pursue. How was such an opportunity created in this case, and what factors bore on its suitability?

7. If you were the story-teller in this case, around what key points would you craft the story?

Story Eight: The Reorganization of Public Works

As with the School of Public Policy and Management, in the Public Works venture described below I was again an intrapreneur, this time working always and only inside the Department of Public Works.

In developing the story I have tried to provide a sense of what life can be like in a large, highly complex organization when you have been employed explicitly to function entrepreneurially. Through the story I address what "functioning entrepreneurially" actually meant in the Public Works context. My focus was on reorganization, and on the revitalization of what the Prime Minister had described to my Deputy Minister as a moribund organization needing to be brought back to life. I had a title, a position that gave me status in the organization and ready access to the Deputy Minister, but little else in the way of direction. My mandate was as nebulous as "lead in reorganizing and revitalizing the Department".

As you read, note particularly the use of the concept, "alter ego" and what it implies in the way of a working and trust relationship. Note, also, how the story introduces a new idea about leadership of a complex entrepreneurial venture, namely that in order to handle the complexity, there can be two lead entrepreneurs to divide the leadership challenge between them.

The Story

When I joined the federal public service, John MacDonald was Deputy Minister of Indian and Northern Affairs Canada. He was known both for his competence as a top manager and for his entrepreneurial approach to social policy issues. When I told him I wanted to spend a year as a federal public servant working on social policy issues he agreed to my joining his department as a policy advisor.

He made it clear, however, that he would not be looking to me for any noteworthy contribution, having concluded after considerable experience with academics that we had very little of practical value to contribute to public service decisions. His approach was: "Join us for a year, Walter. I will see that you have an office, a secretary, and access to our policy materials. You'll get to know from inside how policy is made and how the public service really works. Then you can go back to York with a much stronger background for teaching public policy and management."

Although not at all challenging, this sounded just fine at the time. After three full academic years at Queen's obtaining my doctorate and two hectic years building the School of Public Policy and Management at York, I would have a leisurely year in

Ottawa, browsing around the public service with no pressure to produce. Accordingly, the arrangement was finalized and, as a family, we rented our Thornhill home and relocated to Ottawa for what we believed would be a temporary stay.

This decision to move was not a casual one for the family. Two years earlier we had built an attractive home backing on a golf course, and settled into our new community. The children were all in schools they enjoyed and had made close friends in the neighborhood. Understandably, there were prolonged and sometimes heated family discussions about whether the planned temporary move to Ottawa was wise or whether, as an alternative, I should simply commute for the year.

When we decided to move, we had then to decide what to do about our new home and what to do about accommodation in Ottawa. One result of such discussion was that our oldest child David announced his decision to stay in Thornhill and continue to attend his existing high school, which we ultimately supported. This was not easy for Barbara, seeing the first bird leave the family nest and having to make the required arrangements concerning where he would stay and who would act as temporary guardian.[1]

It was relevant to the discussion that by age 17, David had lived in 17 different locations. Although such mobility was related as much to our various moves while I was attending university as to entrepreneurial ventures, it is by no means a necessary demand of entrepreneurial families that they be frequently on the move.

The first day I arrived in the Department, while still settling in, John strode into my office and said, "Walter, drop everything you're doing. You're a political scientist – we need a policy on governing the Canadian North as soon as you can develop it." He then

---

[1] There is a story I tell in my workshops about an American Congresswoman who, when visiting a refugee camp, struck up a conversation with an eight-year-old girl who had lived there all her life. In the course of the conversation the Congresswoman said to the girl, "It is such a pity you don't have a home!" The girl replied sweetly, "Oh, but we do have a home. We just don't have a house to put it in."

As a family, we were fortunate that Barbara was an excellent homemaker who, in addition to her other contributions to family well-being, was able to move our home readily from house to house.

strode out, leaving me bewildered. I was not even sure I knew what constituted the Canadian North and had not the remotest idea what was required in the way of a policy to govern it. Some minutes later, however, a messenger arrived carrying several red files marked "Secret." After signing for them I closed my office door and began work.

I read the files with interest. It became obvious there was a policy, in embryonic form, emerging from a reading of the files. It had been gestating for the past two years and simply needed to be articulated clearly. The current urgency was that the Minister was facing tough questions in the House of Commons about the government's plans for the North.

There was, however, a major drawback that had prevented finalization of the policy. On being briefed at one point by the committee working on the policy, John had commented that it should be developed around a regional government model. Yet the committee had concluded that a regional government model would not work in the Canadian North. What was needed instead was a municipal model. Yet the Deputy had spoken, and committee members believed themselves obligated to reflect his stated position!

Accordingly, when I found the material in the files to be strongly supportive of the committee's model, I asked John's secretary to book me some time with him. I walked into the meeting, cheerfully, to tell him what I had found. There was a policy, and I could capture it quickly, if only he would move back from his insistence on a regional government model.

I had expected the type of leisurely and stimulating debate I might have carried on with colleagues at York. Instead, I experienced for the first time a powerful Deputy Minister in action. He challenged me immediately and forcefully to justify why he should change his mind. I was not at all prepared with the type of careful, very tight presentation he obviously required, so asked him to let me see him again later in the day.

After briefing him on my return, he agreed the model the committee had developed was the preferred one. Within 10 days I had the policy written for presentation in speeches by the Minister during visits to Whitehorse and Yellowknife.

Had I been asked as an academic to take on the task of preparing a policy on governing Canada's North, my approach would have been markedly different. I would have wanted to assemble a team, carry out some exemplary research including visits to the North, and take the time to develop and write up the policy.

Within the public service, circumstances dictated a different approach.

An influential and outspoken northern MP was harassing the Minister during Question Period, pressing the government to grant provincial status to the Yukon and Northwest Territories. The Minister needed defensible policy within a tight time horizon, therefore, and it was fortunate that the policy direction was simple to discern, prepare and defend through what the Committee had developed.

Over a three-month period John handed me a total of four key policy issues and, on one occasion, a challenging management issue to resolve. I found myself immersed in and thoroughly enjoying a public service milieu far different from that of the university or my earlier experiences in the business sector. It was a particular joy, moreover, to be working closely with someone possessing a fine mind, matching the best I had encountered in university circles – and someone who came to look to me as a tough sounding board on policy issues.

The upshot of all of this was that when the Prime Minister asked John to move from Indian Affairs and Northern Development to the Department of Public Works, which was in need of reorganization, John asked me to move with him. He promised that, if I was willing to leave my university position and commit to what he believed would be four years with the new department, he would begin the process immediately of having my rank raised to that of Assistant Deputy Minister and assign me responsibility for leading the reorganization.

This was a totally unanticipated offer. If accepted, it would take me along a very different career path, at least temporarily. Yet John wanted an immediate answer.

The role the Deputy described was a challenging one, and my total public service experience was only three months. More importantly, when I joined the public service it had been with the intent of this being a step toward a long and satisfying career in the field of social policy and management, taking place primarily in a university environment.

I knew absolutely nothing about the provision of design, construction and property management services and had not the slightest desire to learn. My first strong inclination, therefore, was to decline the offer, finish out my temporary stay with the public service, and return to university even though I was not at all hopeful that the Faculty's decision climate would have changed within the year to support a new School of Social Policy and Management.

John then showed me a five-page letter he had written to the Prime Minister, capturing a new vision for Public Works, and the Prime Minister's cautiously favorable reply. It was an intriguing vision that would raise myriad challenges in its pursuit. Going beyond the correspondence, John told me of his belief that if he and I worked together on the reorganization, it was probable we could develop and manage a public service organization performing at the level of the best comparable organizations in the business sector.

This provided an attractive new perspective on what John had in mind in terms of the role he planned to create for me. I accepted the offer and moved immediately to Public Works, while John stayed a further three months in Indian and Northern Affairs to smooth the transition to his successor.

The Public Works project differed in entrepreneurial challenge from any of my previous ventures. Although I had grown as an entrepreneur on the basis of each successive venture, nothing in my entrepreneurial background seemed directly relevant to the environment of a federal department. A doctorate in Political Studies with an academic specialty in Public Policy and Management was no guarantee I would be able to function at so senior a rank as a practitioner in the federal public service.

I am not certain, looking back, why I was not intimidated by the Public Works challenge. It may have been simply a case of "fools rush in..." The more probable reason was that I had worked for three months with John on major challenges and had felt very comfortable while doing so. I had also learned to respect his judgment about the capabilities of those around him and must have been reassured, sub-consciously, that if he believed I could do the job, then I probably could. As a fourth possibility, I was by that time a seasoned entrepreneur, open to becoming engaged in initiatives that would fully challenge my entrepreneurial capabilities. Even on first acquaintance, this was such a challenge.

Within six months of joining the federal public service, I became an Assistant Deputy Minister, charged by the Deputy Minister with heading the reorganization of a department of 9,000 people located in offices across Canada, working on $800 million in public works projects each year and managing some $20 billion in federal real estate. All I had to do, in my new job, was to act for the Deputy Minister in providing the leadership required to "fix" a department supposedly in dire need of reorganization and renewed vitality.

This was no longer small-scale entrepreneurship. It was intrapreneurship on a large scale, made more challenging by the reality that the Department had to fit effectively into a complex public service and a still more complex Canadian political system.

As with every entrepreneurial initiative, the first challenge was to come to grips with the matter of vision, capturing the organization we wanted to see in place several years hence. John had captured his vision for Public Works in his letter to the Prime Minister.

At one time in its 100-year history and in that of the Board of Works, its pre-Confederation predecessor, Public Works had been involved in the design and construction of Canada's major public works. John was one of a number of senior people who recognized what it had actually become over the years – namely, the federal government's realty agency, mandated to serve other federal departments and agencies with realty services. He envisioned the department being replaced by a Crown corporation which would exist solely to meet the realty needs of federal departments and agencies through projects financed from each department's own budget.

The vision captured in John's five-page letter to the Prime Minister was a broad-brush one. It was my responsibility to take that vision, capture it in the detail required to communicate it effectively, and then test it with key public service and political stakeholders with a view to refining it with John where this proved desirable. This done, I had the task of complementing the vision with a clear set of strategic directions able to guide the resulting change initiatives.

As a tough sounding board to John during the three months I had spent at Indian Affairs, I had needed to be keenly aware of his vision for the department, the manner in which he approached issues, where his priorities lay, his preferences in the writing of memoranda and letters, and so on. I had come to know him so well that I could act for him in many different situations as his alter ego. This ability to represent him well was a major factor, I believe, in his wanting to have me transferred to Public Works with him to play a similar role in that department.

It was a special challenge, when playing the role of John's alter ego in Public Works, to come to grips with where he really intended to take the organization. Once I understood this from his perspective and had fleshed it out, I became the guardian of the ensuing vision, protecting it against the dilution, erosion and misapplication that may have occurred as others sought to implement it.

There was a key role to play, also, in its communication. A vision on paper is not the same as a vision in action, especially when the aim is to reorganize an existing organization in a fundamental way. Visions serve little purpose in major reorganizations until they are communicated effectively to those challenged to pursue them and, of even greater importance, until their support for them is assured.

I spent a total of nine months developing, communicating and, after considerable feedback, refining the details of John's embryonic vision. This included translating it into written form for official review. The Government of Canada's public organizations operate under formal mandates captured, in considerable part, in Acts of Parliament and related statutory instruments. If an organization wants to change its direction in a fundamental way, it needs formal authorization to do so. Such change in direction is followed, in turn, by the preparation of the required amendments to statutes and statutory instruments.

Once we had refined and fleshed out the vision, we moved on its implementation. This took us into each of strategic and operational planning, revisions in organizational structure, reworking terms of reference for managers and staff, and re-classifying positions if necessary. We also moved strongly on the mobilization and effective deployment of the people and the financial and material resources we needed, including allocating the large sums of money that made up our annual revenues.

It was new for me to be thinking and planning in relation to thousands of staff and millions of dollars annually, and challenging to adjust to this. We discovered, for example, that prior to our arrival, Public Works had been spending $80,000 a year on training and development. We increased this immediately to $850,000. Our information-handling budget was $200,000, which we increased to $1.4 million. By the end of my four years with the department, the information budget had reached $4.5 million and was still on a strong growth trajectory, so rapidly were the costs of information growing.

Our managerial cadre was initially 345. Within the first year we raised it to 455 and invested heavily in managerial staffing and development, knowing we were taking the department in a direction that would require a larger group of managers of improved competence. As we created new positions, we had to classify and staff these while moving, in parallel, to eliminate certain positions and to relocate, retrain or release redundant staff.

We began to foster a new leadership philosophy and style, make effective use of team management, and create project teams using a matrix structure. We designed and implemented performance measurement and program evaluation processes at a time when these were making their first appearance in the federal public service, and strengthened the department's internal audit process. We streamlined and strengthened our decision processes and our internal and external communications. We also strengthened significantly our client service orientation and our public relations and public information processes.

I found myself entering into a challenging set of decision processes and networks – and divided among many of them was the power we needed to work our way to successful conclusions. By comparison, my previous ventures in entrepreneurship in the business sector were on a small scale indeed. This was true also in relation to the university initiative. Although York University had proven to be a challenging environment it, too, paled in comparison to that of the federal public service.

We had to know our relevant internal and external environments and be able to function effectively within them. Appropriate champions, allies, supporters and partners had to be identified, and effective relationships with each developed. We had to understand the various decision processes, know how and when to use each for optimum results, and be both tough-minded and resilient in protecting and furthering our reorganization initiatives. As with entrepreneurs working on a much smaller scale, we also had to be light on our feet, willing and able to change direction while still moving forward when events required such flexibility.

Ultimately, we had to be prepared for the possibility that what we were striving so hard to accomplish might not happen because we lacked the required level of competence on some key performance dimension or because unforeseen and/or uncontrollable factors entered the picture. As a case in point: the FLQ crisis in October 1970 emerged out of left field to deny us approval for the conversion of Public Works into the Crown Corporation we had been seeking as a major step toward reorganizing the federal Public Works function. The required proposal to create the Crown Corporation was officially already in the works, and we believed it was progressing toward approval when this internal terrorist threat occurred and swept everything else off the public agenda. Months later, when the federal government was able to resume normal business, our time had passed.

A valuable aspect of the Public Works experience was that I came to understand that entrepreneurial leadership can be shared and, indeed, may need to be. In order to revitalize and reorganize the department so fundamentally, two key and somewhat distinct roles needed to be filled. First, and far and away the more important, was accountability for and leadership of the department as a whole. In relation to the reorganization itself, moreover, someone had to deal with the most senior contacts outside the department. Secondly, and less demanding in terms of political and public service competence but more demanding in terms of the ongoing exercise of entrepreneurial/managerial capability, we had to deal with the internal dimension.

It was this second role that John recognized he could not handle by himself, even though it was implied in the role of Deputy Minister. A major heart attack three years earlier had left him incapable of working at the sustained and highly stressful level it would have required. He did not see the solution being to assign the responsibility for supporting him to a regular senior public servant, recognizing instead that this was more an entrepreneurial challenge than a managerial one.

He functioned as the lead entrepreneur for the overall departmental reorganization, including both political and public service aspects, while situating me in the role of lead entrepreneur for the revitalization process. I believe this arrangement worked because our roles were quite distinct with very little overlap, and were suited to our respective abilities. Without it being spelled out, I functioned as his alter ego throughout.

For the first time I was working with and under the overall guidance of a proven creative entrepreneur. John had committed himself to leading a major reorganization of the Department. Except in John's mind, I was nowhere formally in the picture when he made this commitment. This said, by making me personally and directly accountable to him for heading the reorganization internally, and by giving me the authority and freedom to do so, he put me in the position of a lead entrepreneur.

In comparison with my own accountability for leading initiatives of an internal management nature, John was playing the role only he could play. He was dealing with the Minister, other Ministers and their respective senior political advisors, the Privy Council Office, the Prime Minister's Office, and his own top-level public service counterparts including those in the central agencies and major client departments. John represented the department in the most senior and sensitive decision forums outside the strictly-political arena. He was the department's Chief Executive Officer and, for John, delegation was never abdication. However much he chose to leave to me to head the reorganization and revitalization or to the three other assistant deputy ministers who were heading the Department's ongoing programs, he stayed very aware of what each of his top managers was doing.

Four years into the reorganization, we had worked our way through all that was feasible of what we had planned and were at the point where the Department needed to settle down and consolidate. I had been focused strictly on forward-looking revitalization and, after four years, we had strong people in place who were capable of settling the Department down in its new form and managing its ongoing activities. Accordingly, I judged my job to be over. John was not of the same mind, foreseeing policy and management issues arising I could usefully address. He did agree, however, that "Project Renewal," as we had called our revitalization initiative, could be terminated.

When I told John I wanted to move back into the field of social policy and management, he offered me the chance to take advantage of a generous sabbatical program available at the time to senior public servants. It involved continuing on full salary and having all expenses paid to study for a year anywhere in the world. When I declined the offer, he advised me to enter the federal language program to prepare myself for a permanent position at a senior level in one of the social policy departments, and this advice I accepted. I completed the language program but there were no suitable openings. When the Chair of the Public Service Commission asked John to loan me to the Commission to head an initiative in Executive Education, John agreed, and for several months I was the head of Executive Education for the federal public service. This was not a happy experience. The Chair was far from being a John MacDonald. The chemistry between us was poor and I experienced, for the first time, what life could be like for a creative entre-preneur locked into a relentlessly bureaucratic environment.

Fortunately, a short time into my new role I was asked to represent the Commission on a task force established to explore the feasibility and desirability of establishing a National School of Public Administration in Ottawa. Such a National School seemed to make little sense, given the federal nature of Canada and the existence of several good schools or departments of public administration in key provincial locations across Canada.

Accordingly, I urged the task force to change direction and support an initiative that would see several university-based Schools of Public Policy and Management, mandated by the federal government to educate its managers and financially supported to help accomplish this.

Such regionally-located schools, I argued, could provide the required professional education not only to those destined for positions in the federal public service but also for those planning to work in provincial, territorial or local public services. I recommended, further, that we set up a bilingual prototype in Ottawa, through a joint initiative of Carleton University and the University of Ottawa. The task force endorsed these proposals.

The Dean of the Faculty of Administration from the University of Ottawa was on the task force. Shortly afterward, the Dean offered me the position of Chairman of the Faculty's Department of Public Administration, together with a tenured position as Professor of Public Policy and Management. He assured me, further, that I would have his full support and cooperation in establishing the joint University of Ottawa/Carleton University School of Public Policy and Management. I accepted the offer, and ended my five-year public service career.

I left the public service knowing a great deal more about how the Government of Canada and its public service functioned. Having made numerous speeches over the five-year period and led many workshops, seminars and conferences, I was taking with me a wealth of teaching materials and very useful contacts. These would stand me in good stead in a professional faculty where both consulting and executive education outside the university were encouraged.

Commentary

1. A difference between intrapreneurship and entrepreneurship which bears on environmental factors is highlighted in this story. John MacDonald is portrayed as a successful intrapreneur. He had proven this in other federal departments in addition to Indian Affairs and Northern Development, and Public Works. Yet he would not have performed as competently in the role of entrepreneur. His stock-in-trade was his exceptionally fine understanding

of and ability to work within the special environment of the federal public service within the Canadian political system.

2. He understood this environment intimately in all its complexity, and applied a brilliant mind throughout his career to resolving the challenges it presented. He understood the politics of a public service environment intuitively, and was a master at the art of generating workable compromises among influential power-holders seeking a common direction. Of particular importance, he had an exceptional sense of public service as a calling. He was proud to be a public servant and had no interest in becoming involved in business.

3. Although complex and multilayered, the environment John worked within had identifiable boundaries, its own culture and traditions, its particular decision processes, and its special power-holders and stakeholders.

    Compared to most organizations in the private sector, enormous resources could be made available to John if he could make the case for these. Although private sector entrepreneurs skilled in the art of raising capital can also access large amounts of funding for their projects, John's resourcing skills were related to public sector budgetary processes that differ markedly from private sector financing.

4. In contrast, the environment of the entrepreneur has no such established boundaries. The entrepreneur's challenge, working outside existing organizations, is to find a niche that no organization has yet identified or filled satisfactorily and create the organization that will fill the niche effectively. There will be no internal environment until the new organization has been created. As a consequence, it is a challenge for the entrepreneur to identify and then manage relevant aspects of the external environment, starting with little more than an idea.

5. The willingness and ability to "speak truth" to those in positions of power was instrumental in generating the Public Works opportunity. John MacDonald needed someone to function as a reliable sounding board against which to test his ideas and whom he could trust to give frank and informed advice, despite his own well-known penchant for hard-driving responses to such advice

if it was difficult to accept. John's mind moved so well and quickly, and he worked from so finely-developed a sense of how the federal government did and should function, that his senior managers tended to deny him the tough critique he needed to challenge some decisions he had to make.

6. To play the role of influential sounding board requires both willingness and ability. Willingness was no problem in my case. It was relatively easy for me to provide that sounding board. It certainly helped our relationship that I was initially on leave from the university and could speak more freely than might have been possible had I been a regular member of John's staff. What was harder for me, coming as I did from an environment where tact and sensitivity in discussions with university colleagues was neither particularly treasured nor required, was to acquire the ability to critique his ideas with appropriate sensitivity to his undeniable decision strengths and his position as the Department's top executive and the Minister's chief advisor on policy.

7. Experienced entrepreneurs only consider especially-challenging opportunities seriously when they are convinced they can address them effectively. It is one thing to move on an exciting challenge. It is quite another to tackle something beyond our ability. John's proposal that I head the reorganization became a genuine entrepreneurial opportunity only when I could see myself being effective in the role he had in mind for me.

8. Chemistry and environmental fit are important to entrepreneurial success. The chemistry with John MacDonald was exceptionally good in Public Works, and the special regard in which I came to hold him made it easy for me to assume the role of his alter ego in organization revitalization initiatives. Then, too, the Public Works environment was a dynamic one and we were committed to moving the Department forward at a challenging speed, which suited my temperament well.

9. Public Works was an environment in which I could function at peak entrepreneurial capacity, but this was not the case with the Public Service Commission. Creative intrapreneurs will not work equally well in all situations and some ventures on which we embark are best moved away from as quickly as

possible. When the likelihood of making a significant contribution is low, and our entrepreneurial juices are flowing sluggishly, if at all, it is time to move on as graciously as possible.

10. Previously, mention was made of how important it is for the intrapreneur to have an effective champion. In the Public Works story this is expanded to include a reference to the value also of "allies, supporters and partners." When working within an organization where the power to decide is shared among numerous decision-makers, it is essential to draw upon sympathetic power-holders in cobbling together the power required to ensure a favorable decision.

11. This story brings into focus the key issue of security. Both entrepreneurs and intrapreneurs tend to value security less highly than normal. If they did not, they would be unable to take the security risks that are part of their respective worlds. One of Pinchot's intrapreneurship commandments is "Come to work every day prepared to be fired." (1985) Following this introduces a significant degree of insecurity into the intrapreneurs' work environment. Yet entrepreneurship also has additional stressors.

12. The more security-conscious may be drawn to intrapreneurship because of its positive benefits in relation to providing a more secure income. In my entrepreneurial ventures, there were times when our personal finances were barely adequate to cover our most basic needs. This was a price I necessarily and willingly paid for the freedom to be an entrepreneur, although it would be misleading to suggest that Barbara was always equally as willing.

13. The insecurity in relation to personal finances extends beyond wages or salary. In start-up situations and whenever capital is extremely short, everything that normally accumulates to establish "net personal worth" can be put at risk when all we own has been contributed to building value into a business that has yet to prove itself. Link this to the lack of medical, dental and pension benefits, and it becomes starkly clear how much can be put at risk in the pursuit of entrepreneurial visions. Now compare that to having the excellent salary and related benefits that go with working in a large organization as a successful intrapreneur, and it can be seen that the differences are profound.

14. A major challenge for entrepreneurs is to find the resources their ventures require. Many larger organizations, however, have rich resource bases and can channel significant resources to attractive revitalization initiatives. In the Public Works venture, for example, we were able to find within healthy budgets millions of dollars for the new directions we wanted to take. If such directions related in some identifiable way to broader public service goals, we were able to draw upon significant additional funding from the federal treasury. Neither was development capital a problem in the York University venture. The proviso in relation to both ventures was that we needed to understand the politics of the internal budgetary processes and work capably with these.

15. It is not always the case, however, that the resources for a particular initiative will be found more readily within an organization than outside. There are plenty of examples of creative people who, having tried without success to move their ideas forward within an organization, have opted to move out of it to find greater support for their initiatives in the outside environment.

16. There is a difference worth noting between intrapreneurship and entrepreneurship in relation to the sources of power from which each draws. As entrepreneurs, our power comes in important part from ourselves. Drawing on this power we will identify an entrepreneurial opportunity, develop and refine our vision, and pursue that vision to create a new reality. As entrepreneurs, we chart the directions we want to take, draw around us the people we need to support us, mobilize needed resources, and apply those resources to complete the implementation action required to make our visions real.

    We will draw significant additional power from the contributions of those working with us: our partners if any; our financiers; the professional support we receive from lawyers and accountants; our suppliers; the staff we employ; and the personal support from our family and involved friends and colleagues. It is we, however, who will make the decisions on what power we seek to obtain, from whom, and under what arrangements – and throughout, we will be working to create the new organization required to realize our vision. Our contact with existing organizations will be primarily as sources of power in the special roles we need them to play.

17. As intrapreneurs, we still draw a great deal of the power we need from ourselves and, in this regard, the nature of such power is similar to that of the entrepreneur. Yet the power we need and which is potentially available to us will be drawn, in considerable measure, also from inside the organizations of which we are members. To draw upon that power effectively we have to learn what power resides with those who occupy which particular positions in the organization. There will be those whose positions we need to influence, and our intervention could well be viewed negatively. As intrapreneurs, we have to be particularly sensitive to such realities.

18. Although there is abundant room in intrapreneurship for creative thinkers who question the status quo and can put forward positive, practical alternatives, there is normally no useful place for extreme anti-bureaucratic mavericks who lack the capacity to make needed accommodations to organizational life.

Questions to Consider

1. What is implied by the phrase "Speaking Truth to Power" and how was it important in this case?

2. What is the meaning and significance to the Public Works venture of the concept of "alter ego"?

3. Why must entrepreneurs provide leadership in evolving the vision to be pursued, but also lead in both communicating it and protecting it "from erosion, dilution and misapplication?"

4. Why, in this story, was it especially critical that the vision be captured in writing in both "broad-brush" and detailed form?

5. How is having two lead entrepreneurs presented and defended in the story? What do you believe was pivotal in making it work?

6. Why did I initially plan to reject the offer to head up the reorganization/revitalization of the Department, and what then drew me in? What is the significance of this for entrepreneurship in general?

7.   How important do you believe the issue of security is to you personally, and would the value you place on security cause you to seek a career as an intra-preneur rather than entrepreneur? Is the security concern sufficiently strong that you may find yourself avoiding the risks of both intrapreneurship and entrepreneurship?

Story Nine: Shaping the Future - Canada in a Global Society

It may seem an anti-climax to end this chapter with a story covering a venture that lasted only six months from the first glimmering of an idea to the organization and delivery of an International Conference and Futures Fair, especially when presented following immediately after the Public Works venture. A great deal of entrepreneurial activity was compressed into a tight schedule.

Although particularly short, the story has been included in the series for three reasons:

- First, it shows that when we identify a need we want to see met through our efforts and which can only be met by creating a new organization, that organization does not have to be permanent. If a new organization is needed to achieve a clearly-articulated short-term goal we judge worth pursuing, then building the organization to reach that goal would be an entrepreneurial accomplishment, even when we disband the organiza-tion shortly thereafter.

- Second, the story is an example of the entrepreneur having to work through a committee, thereby constraining the entrepreneur's individ-ual freedom to decide while giving useful support. Committee members representing powerful organizations had to be brought together to meet the goal. Leadership, however, had to be provided by an entrepre-neur functioning initially as a negotiator and facilitator, and able to give the additional time this required, even while committing to tight dead-lines and high performance standards.

- Third, there is a parallel with creating the Advisory Board for the School of Public Policy and Management. Deliberately bringing into this venture such prestigious partners as we did required that we set and maintain high quality standards in all aspects of the Conference – again, in full knowledge of the tight time-lines.

The Story

Four years into my University of Ottawa career an entrepreneurial opportunity of short duration arose. I was asked if I would chair the annual conference of the Canadian Association of Futures' Studies (CAFS). This was at a time when futures institutes were springing up around the world and earnest attempts to predict the future were in vogue.

I agreed to do so on two conditions: first, that we establish the title as, "Shaping the Future: Canada in a Global Society"; and, secondly, that I be allowed to bring together with CAFS, as sponsors, each of the Science Council of Canada, the Economic Council of Canada, the Institute for Research on Public Policy, and the Club of Rome as co-sponsors. In this way, I believed, we could mount a significant initiative to address a vital social challenge. CAFS and the sponsors came together around this, and we arranged that the Conference would be held at the University of Ottawa in August when there would be plenty of conference and residential space available at relatively low cost.

We assembled a ten-member Conference Committee to focus on strategic directions and ensure strategic coordination across Conference-member boundaries. Over a six-month period we organized and delivered five parallel conferences on major sub-themes and organized a follow-up Futures Fair. We identified and recruited 79 distinguished speakers from Canada and around the world as well as chairs, commentators, panel members, and facilitators for the various sessions. We also booked a considerable number of conference, break-out and workshop rooms; prepared and distributed required publicity materials; arranged for catering-- and so on, to cover the many planned conference and Futures Fair activities.

The Conference attracted some 1,800 participants over the three conference days. This was followed, on the fourth morning, by a closing session which provided an overview of what had been discussed during the Conference, preparing the overview from the large number of tape recordings and notes taken during the many sessions.

After the Conference, it was also our task to see to the development and distribution of a 700- page set of Conference Proceedings. Given the amount of editing and original writing required, producing the Proceedings was a challenge in its own right.

As a final happening, reflecting the significance of the venture, towards the end of the Conference, the Privy Council Office requested that we brief them on our findings and conclusions.

Although lasting only six months from the initial suggestion to the distribution of the proceedings, this qualified as an entrepreneurial venture. Beginning with an unformed idea, we had to envision what might be created if everything were to come together effectively within the time available. The vision had to be capable of filling an exciting social niche, and be compelling and realistic enough to be able to mobilize the needed resources. The Conference Committee had to commit to it strongly if we were to provide the entrepreneurial spark and sustain it over the length of the venture. We also had to be able to communicate the vision and win the commitment and support of those who needed to be involved and, subsequently, to provide leadership of a nature that would generate, harness and maintain the required energy.

We had to bring into being a new organization, temporarily, and manage it effectively in order to meet clear goals and operational objectives. The vision was ambitious enough to create a formidable challenge that carried with it the risk that, by seeking to achieve so much in so short a period, we might produce, instead, a lackluster event fraught with resource and administrative difficulties.

I was working with a decision committee made up of representatives of powerful strategic partners. Until key decisions were made on where we were heading and with what end result we had in mind, my role was that of negotiator and facilitator, drawing together from the initial visions a common one that incorporated the insights and preferences of Conference Committee members.

Such members were understandably intent on ensuring that what we produced was consistent with the mandates of their respective organizations and reflected positively on them. Inherent in this set of negotiator/facilitator challenges was the special challenge of bringing together, harmoniously, those differing greatly in their perspectives on and approaches to the challenge of shaping the future. Scientists and economists are uneasy colleagues with futures associations and environmental activists who are intent on shaking up the establishment.

Commentary

1. There was no thought, as we worked together, of using the Conference as a springboard into the establishment of a Canadian futures centre active in the worldwide community of futures organizations.

    Such a potential outcome was indeed there and I will show, later, that the Conference did lead for me, personally, to a major entrepreneurial opportunity arising from nothing more complicated than taking Conference volunteers into the country for a barbecue. The organization we created to design, develop and deliver a successful international conference and futures fair, however, was disbanded shortly after the event. As the story notes, organizations created by entrepreneurs are not always intended to be permanent.

2. Committees like the one featured in the story will not become, jointly, the entrepreneur. Rather, it takes an entrepreneur, in the first place, to develop the initial vision and related story that will bring the required partners willingly into the venture. Once assembled, they tend to become similar to the Board of Directors of a regular corporate organization and to function at a strategic decision level as in this story.

3. At the very minimum, partner participation brought immediate credibility to the venture. Additionally, partners were an important source of funding and other resources. It was up to me to then move ahead entrepreneurially in pursuit of the established goals. In this case, in addition to the 10 people on the Conference Committee, we assembled 150 volunteers as the essential resource base for ensuring the Conferences and follow-up Futures Fair took place successfully.

4. Once again, as was the case with the School of Public Policy and Management, I saw this new venture starting from a request by someone else that I take on organizational responsibilities; in this case, to chair an annual futures' conference. From that point I moved to win the commitment to a much more

demanding and exciting event involving a much higher level of entrepreneurial risk for a sizeable gain in value.

Questions to Consider

5. What was the risk element in the venture and how do you believe it was handled?

6. Do you agree that this was "a significant initiative to address a vital social challenge"? If so, can you see how it would be relatively straightforward to find other social challenges able to be addressed through bringing an International Conference together successfully – and can you see, also, that each such initiative would require drawing on entrepreneurial capability?

7. In relation to what elements of the venture was leadership a major success factor and what particular leadership style was required?

8. Why would we have chosen a university campus as the venue for our conference, and what would have been the significance of scheduling it in August?

Entrepreneurs and Status

It might be useful at this point to make some observations about the role status plays in entrepreneurial success or in its impact on the relative attractiveness of intrapreneurship and entrepreneurship. During several of my ventures as an entrepreneur I was also a graduate student. In the case of Echo Park when I was no longer a student, I was someone with no capital to contribute to the venture and nothing to bring to it but entrepreneurial ability.

We need a strong ego and be comfortable in ourselves if we are to thrive in an environment in which we are at least initially without major status. This is especially so when we are dealing with shareholders we have brought together who are people of prestige in the community.

In our intrapreneurial situations, also, we may be operating above what might more normally have been our level in the organization. This could prove challenging because of the possible concern of colleagues and others who are climbing the hierarchical ladder only slowly and with considerable focused effort. It will work if we are at ease in the positions we have acquired or been given and take the increased status in our stride. The value of being at a more elevated level will be the greater access it provides to senior decision makers and to resources.

As a creative entrepreneur, it helps if you are comfortable both with and without status. If you need the trappings of formal authority to do your best work, then seek to situate yourself inside an organization. The best organizations can be a rich source of advice, protection and support from people who share a commitment to the organization's vision. Inside such organizations, moreover, the freedom lost from having someone oversee our work is more than compensated for by the security and support an effective manager can bring to our venture.

If we thrive in such an environment, we may not want to leave the warm security of the organization to function on our own in a world lacking organizational supports. That is just fine because the organization itself may prove to be an exciting environment within which to apply our entrepreneurial capability. Yet some of you, I know, will opt for the role of entrepreneur and be productive in such a role. You will want the special challenges of being an entrepreneur in building a new organization and being fully prepared for a world where you may be functioning without special status.

CHAPTER FOUR
Strathmere and the Entrepreneurial Process

Notwithstanding its special creativity, flexibility and susceptibility to chance, there is nothing haphazard about successful entrepreneurship, whether taking place inside or outside an organization. On the contrary, there is implicit in all but the simplest of ventures a common entrepreneurial process followed more or less systematically from recognition that we may have found an entrepreneurial opportunity meriting our attention.

In this Chapter, through Story 10, I describe how we found the entrepreneurial opportunity, "Strathmere." Stories 11 and 12 then take us through the exploration and acquisition of Strathmere and its development into a family business. Although the International Conference had been of short duration, and an instance of entrepreneurship on a small scale, it led in this way to an entrepreneurial initiative of sizeable proportions.

Story Ten: Strathmere Becomes an Entrepreneurial Opportunity

150 volunteers had worked to bring the Shaping the Future Conference and companion Futures Fair into being. Wanting to acknowledge everyone's contribution to a successful collaborative venture, and believing that an outdoor barbecue would be an appropriate way to do so, we cast around for a suitable country setting. Someone on our Conference Team mentioned Strathmere, a 400-acre personal growth centre modeled after a

European folk school, located 30 km from the center of downtown Ottawa and 12 km from Ottawa's international airport. Alex and Eleanor Sim, the owners, were involved in the futures movement and had attended the Conference and Fair. Accordingly, on their invitation that is where we went for the barbecue.

Described in a local history as one of the Ottawa Valley's finest historic farms, Strathmere consisted of a 6,000 square foot pre-Confederation stone farmhouse known as Strathmere House; two large barns in decrepit shape; a large chicken house, also in decrepit shape; an historic one-room schoolhouse; acres of meadows, and many additional acres of farmland in active use for raising the Centre's own crops.

Several weeks earlier, Barbara and I had been at Chateau Montebello in Quebec, where I was leading a management workshop. At the time I was active on the management development circuit, travelling from venue to venue across Canada and occasionally abroad. Over breakfast, Barbara remarked that it would be a relief to her if I could hold the bulk of my workshops at a local site so that I travelled less. I responded enthusiastically, seeing the possibility of acquiring a site which, in addition to being close to home, could be transformed into an ideal setting for management and organizational development and related hospitality services.

I saw Strathmere immediately as such a possible site. While everyone else was eating, therefore, I had Alex Sim show me around. As we walked, I asked him whether he had any thought of selling the property. It turned out he had been exploring the prospects of a sale since he turned 70, two years earlier, and had settled on a price of $400,000. He told me also that, although the land was zoned agricultural, the property had a special zoning exemption that covered his growth centre and other educational activities, tourism and a summer camp.

This brief conversation initiated a complex, challenging entrepreneurial process which extended over 2-3 years as we moved to explore, acquire and develop the facility. The following pages outline this process in detail as it developed at Strathmere, over time, into a successful family venture.

The Entrepreneurial Process

There were several phases for the entrepreneurial process we followed, starting as we did from a preliminary idea that Strathmere might prove attractive as a new entrepreneurial opportunity.

Phase 1 Background

The entrepreneurial process begins with an individual, operating alone or with a group, who has been prepared by life and possibly by particular learning experiences for identifying and responding to entrepreneurial opportunities. I was the entrepreneur for this particular process and looking, at the time, for an interesting opportunity.

Phase 2 Finding a possible opportunity

An entrepreneur becomes aware of the need for goods and/or services that is either not being met at all through existing organizations or, in the individual's judgment, is not being met as well as he or she judges possible. Through the barbecue I had my first introduction to Strathmere as such an opportunity.

Phase 3 A Preliminary Interest

In the walk-around with Alec Sim I was already experiencing a preliminary interest in Strathmere as a possible entrepreneurial opportunity. If the opportunity was to proceed still further, however, my interest needed to grow much stronger. A clearer identification and refinement of the opportunity was needed, with this growing in turn into a vision of the sought-after end result.

Phase 4 Growing into a Compelling Vision

The vision became and remained compelling. As the interested entrepreneur, I moved beyond preliminary interest toward solid pursuit of the vision. I was prepared for a challenging entrepreneurial venture and was able to identify and assess the opportunity on the basis of considerable entrepreneurial experience.

Yet there was something of a more fundamental nature than experience alone. What was involved in the way of personal attributes, background and experience that caused me to take on the risks associated with an entrepreneurial venture of significant size and complexity? I was reasonably fulfilled by my university and management consulting roles in relation to career challenges. Yet here I was, once again, seriously considering an entrepreneurial venture I could expect to be severely under-capitalized from the outset.

A partial answer is that, at the age of 17, I had moved into entrepreneurship without any direct experience of what was involved, or any felt motivation to be a creative entrepreneur. Having moved into it, however, I had found entrepreneurship to be interesting and congenial. I had learned that I possessed the right mindset and entrepreneurial spirit, and had taken on progressively more challenging ventures and grown from each. I was, by this time, an experienced entrepreneur ready to explore an interesting opportunity.

Phase 5 Clarifying the Entrepreneurial Opportunity

This phase of the process consisted of two key elements. First, in relation to Strathmere we needed to identify a viable market opportunity in what we believed could be a highly competitive marketplace. Secondly, having done so, we needed to ensure the opportunity was attractive given our personal and family circumstances, skills, values, and interests.

We had to see Strathmere as more than just a great place to own, assuming we were to acquire it. I had no interest in becoming a member of the landed gentry, strolling around the acreage with a couple of dogs and a sturdy walking stick. The land and buildings had to be the capital base for a profitable commercial venture, or we had to raise the funds to operate a not-for-profit venture on the site.

If we chose the business alternative – as we did – there had to be a niche (an opening) in a competitive market for a use we could foresee. The market niche we identified for Strathmere had to be one I wanted to fill with so deep a desire that the venture would engage me strongly and focus my creative energy. I was experienced enough to have a realistic sense of the sustained effort that would be required to develop the buildings, grounds, programs and services to support a successful business venture.

I could foresee all too clearly, also, the size of the challenge we would be taking in finding the capital required to support us in buying the property and operating it throughout the initial years of insufficient revenue.

Walking through the buildings and around the acreage with Alex Sim, however, produced an almost instantaneous sense that we had stumbled on a prospective venture on which we could focus our energy and that would bring us considerable joy.

Even on first sight I had no doubt whatsoever that, if we decided to do so, we could acquire the property. Nor did I doubt that, once acquired, we could transform it as a family into something worthy of a full commitment. Yet this sense of certainty was driven more by the heart and soul than the mind. Because of this, we had to prove it to ourselves on a rational level.

A Special Challenge

There was a special challenge in relation to Strathmere that had been absent in my previous entrepreneurial initiatives. When I showed the property to Barbara, I assured her we would not move ahead to acquire it unless she gave the venture her blessing in advance.

By this time in our lives Barbara had been involved with me in a number of educational and entrepreneurial initiatives. These had been unsettling and, on several occasions, had a sizeable element of risk.

For the 10 years prior to Strathmere, our lives had been free of entrepreneurial stress. We had lived in our own house in a fine subdivision. I held salaried positions, first as a senior public servant and then as a university professor and management consultant. We had an excellent annual income and I enjoyed what I was doing. Yet, here I was, once again, thinking seriously about taking on a challenging venture that would absorb much of our time and all our surplus revenue for years into the future.

Barbara did agree to go ahead, however, although on one condition: unlike previous entrepreneurial ventures, I would not share control with outside investors. As a family, therefore, we would come to have and retain majority ownership rights in Strathmere.

By the time the Strathmere opportunity emerged, we had lived in over 25 different houses or apartments. There is an article that explores the differences between "cosmopolitans" who can move at the drop of a hat and establish themselves in new situations without distress, and "locals" who have a strong preference for stability in relation to jobs and physical location. I was the prototype cosmopolitan. Barbara was, without question, a local. Given this background, I had no difficulty agreeing to Barbara's condition that, should we become principal owners of Strathmere, we would exercise effective control and profit from its surplus revenues when these began to be generated. This condition, however, limited our financing options severely.

In the past I had been far more interested in seeing ventures succeed than in ownership rights. When I had given up part-ownership to raise required capital it had been perfectly fine with me. It would have been relatively simple at the time, moreover, because of the contacts developed during the "Shaping the Future" conference, to have brought in colleagues to share ownership of Strathmere. Had we done so, I would have been in and out of the venture within a two-to-three-year period of vigorous entrepreneurial activity, leaving the subsequent settling down and ongoing management of what we created to those better suited to managing an established business.

Phase 6 Moving Closer to Commitment

With Barbara's agreement that we should explore taking on the venture, it was now propitious from a personal perspective. I had the needed professional background and experience, and found the opportunity attractive. It was, moreover, a prospective venture that would not require a career change. It was time to further flesh out the vision and undertake the research necessary to determine if we could bring that vision to life.

Story Eleven: Formulating the Vision

When we first identified Strathmere as a prospective entrepreneurial venture, it was in the form of a general idea, only, of where it might take us. I had a sense, only – but a good one – that it might be an opportunity I wanted to pursue. Such an initial sense is all that is required to start the process of visioning, which is one of the most productive elements of entrepreneurship.

We could already envision Strathmere as the base for a futures centre and a compatible centre for management and organizational development. What was now required was a far better sense of what the two centres would look like, once in place, and not only as a set of physical facilities. Before we could commit to their acquisition and development we had to envision them as functioning entities in a dynamic and highly competitive marketplace.

Where our visioning took us, ultimately, was toward the two compatible and complementary niches we had foreseen initially. They would come together into a world class learning centre and meeting venue, situated in a superb setting close to a prime clientele and supported by the required professional staff and excellent hospitality services.

This vision was a compelling one. We appeared to have found a niche that was propitious in a marketing sense, although this had yet to be tested through market research. It was propitious, also, in terms of being a strong fit with our experience and skill sets and, more fundamentally, with family considerations and with who we were and what we valued highly.

An Option to Purchase

Based on experience, we knew not to commit totally to Strathmere on the strength of an attractive vision alone. We did need to make at least a sufficiently strong preliminary commitment, however, to test the feasibility and appropriateness of the identified market niche, and to firm up and refine the vision. Only when this was done would we know whether to put the possible venture behind us or, alternatively, to make the total commitment we would need if we were to move on the venture in a way that gave it much better than a fighting chance of succeeding.

In relation to Strathmere I made such a preliminary commitment readily, after visiting the property several times and talking the possibility over within the family and with colleagues. Accordingly, I went back to meet with Alex Sim shortly after the barbecue, and took with me an "Option to Purchase" we had created.

Such an option is useful in negotiations of this size and type; it brings a special legitimacy and adds important parameters to the serious discussions we will shortly be having, but limits our commitment until we see where discussion of the option takes us.

The Option

- Alex would sign back to me a letter I had prepared, in which he would give me three months to pay him $5,000 for an Option to Purchase. The option would be to buy the 200 acres of land on which the buildings were situated for $250,000, with a five-year option to buy the remaining 200 acres for $200,000. We never exercised this second option.

- We would pay an additional $20,000 nine months after acquiring the original $5,000 Option to Purchase, at which time we would have the right to occupy the farm for a year. During the subsequent year we would be tenants only, renting the farm for $1,000 a month plus carrying the costs of utilities. At the end of the tenancy year we would pay Alex a further $25,000 to a total of $50,000 as down payment on a regular Agreement of Purchase and Sale, and he would take back a $200,000 mortgage amortized over 25 years, with annual compound interest of 6%.

- As a further condition, we would have the right to make improvements to the property during the tenancy year provided Alex, in turn, had the right to approve each change in advance. If we did not pay $25,000 of the down payment on schedule, all improvements would revert to him at no cost and he would keep the $25,000 paid to secure tenancy.

Alex signed the Option to Purchase. At that point no finances had changed hands. Yet for the commitment to pay $5,000 within three months we had obtained the right to buy a 200-acre property including all buildings at an acceptable price of $250,000. By *holding off closing on a purchase for some 21 months, moreover, we had delayed paying mortgage interest and taxes, paying instead only $12,000 for the 12 month tenancy.*

The overriding consideration, however, was that we had obtained not only the time for careful exploration of the possible venture, but also purchase terms that would enable us to buy Strathmere from my consulting income and through its own revenues generated gradually as we moved ahead toward our ultimate vision.

Action Research

The incremental decision-making process gave us close to two years to firm up our commitment, during which time we would have the right to decide whether to move ahead with a final purchase. Given what was at stake, moreover, such review had to be thorough.

It was not the commitment of the $5,000 to obtain the Option to Purchase that was of concern, or even of the $20,000 that would gain us tenancy of the property. These were small enough amounts that to lose them would have been a minor matter – although at many points in my earlier entrepreneurial ventures it would have seemed to be a lot to risk. It was, rather, the commitment to pursue the venture, unrelentingly, giving it everything we could in the expectation we would take it to a successful conclusion. So, the action research component of the process needed to be taken seriously, and final commitment delayed until the research had been completed. It is important that we were prepared to walk away from the venture if objective fact-finding and analysis did not support a decision to proceed.

As the action research phase progressed, there emerged an increasing sense of whether the prospective venture should be pursued or set aside. That sense was in the direction of proceeding; a solid belief in the rightness of the venture was beginning to take hold, and with this came a firming up of commitment. We began to see Strathmere as having strong possibilities in the marketplace and, of even greater importance, to be right for us. We found our minds combining with our hearts and souls into a decision to proceed, and to do so with the passionate commitment so valuable to successful entrepreneurship.

There was a sharpening sense that we were moving toward the reality we had been targeting as the final shape of a new organization. Although there was the making of a solid commitment to proceed with the venture, this did not mean we were now un-swervingly committed to a path from which we would never stray. Nor did it mean we would not end the venture at some future date before we reached our goals. The nature of entrepreneurship is such that we move flexibly and creatively in entrepreneurial response to what we encounter – and this may include changing our vision in minor or major part. What it did mean, however, was that the full force of our entrepreneurial ability was now focused on achieving our vision as we saw it.

Phase 7 Making a Solid Commitment
Pre-implementation and its Challenges

In addition to what can be challenging implementation demands, there are the special advance challenges of readying ourselves for such implementation. There is a process at work, starting with an idea entertained perhaps only fuzzily at first and that could well disappear from the mind after progressing no further. At times, however, the idea will strike some responsive chord and start to grow and sharpen, blossoming into a vision formulated in the mind's eye that had moved considerably beyond the original idea.

As the entrepreneur developing the Strathmere opportunity and judging during the pre-implementation phase that the idea was sufficiently developed, I was ready to share it with those able to critique it usefully. I believe that this sharing stage is important for two reasons. First, it compels me to sharpen the idea in readiness for sharing. Secondly, once it is in presentable form and being shared with colleagues, friends, family, and at some point with potential investors, it will normally add a new level of concreteness to the vision. Questions and comments from others to whom the vision has been exposed and my response to these will compel me to focus strongly on what I am sharing and sharpen a vision still only lodged in my mind.

Finally, as the vision becomes clearer and takes firm hold, I will be in a position to prepare the story I will use in seeking to bring others into the entrepreneurial venture with me.

It will have been one thing to test out my preliminary ideas with friends and colleagues while still bringing everything together only in my head. It is quite another to seek out actual collaborators or partners for the venture who will need to know much more fully what the proposed venture is all about as an important step toward evaluating it.

I will need to become a storyteller, using the story to convey the vision to others who need to see it outside the limited boundaries of my mind's eye. This will become an important step in the process of moving from a preliminary idea into the first stages of actual implementation. There will be nothing casual about it or about the pre-implementation process that precedes it.

A vital component of the essence of entrepreneurship, then, is a pre-implementation process that could extend from nothing more than a first gleam in our eyes, to a creative idea subsequently shaped into an entrepreneurial insight and then growing into a clear vision of where we plan to head. Over still further time and challenging involvement, the pre-implementation process begins to move toward implementation by taking at least preliminary organizational form to support planned implementation.

In terms of capital we will have invested virtually nothing but our time. Yet throughout this pre-implementation phase we will be functioning as creative entrepreneurs, needing to draw strongly on our entrepreneurial competence if the pre-implementation phase is to be a success.

Phase 8   Converting the Vision into Reality

To this point, we had identified an entrepreneurial opportunity, explored the opportunity hard-headedly, formulated an exciting vision of a possible new organization able to fill its own particular niche, and communicated the vision to others we wanted to have join us and inspired them to do so. In the process, we had developed a solid commitment to pursuing the vision. We needed now to expand beyond this to undertake what was required to move from our vision to the reality it foreshadowed.

Story Twelve: Implementation

We had occupied Strathmere at the beginning of the tenancy year. Once the first $25,000 had been paid, and we were able to occupy the property, all we had really purchased was the right to move on our organization-building challenges. Yet by the end of the tenancy year we had spent $50,000 on Alex-approved improvements so that, prior to assuming ownership, we were well- launched into the implementation stage and – including the down payment – had $100,000 at risk with, as yet, no offsetting equity.

$100,000 at risk with no offsetting equity indicates something important about the entrepreneurial mind and spirit. From the moment we moved into residence at Strathmere we were committed to completing the venture unless something strongly negative emerged prior to the end of the second year while we still had the opportunity to back off from acquiring the property. We had arranged the delay of two years from our first payment to the transfer of the property in major part to make it feasible to finance the down payment and initial development from my income.

Prior to the Strathmere implementation phase of the entrepreneurial process we were acquiring 200 acres of property having only one commercial building of value toward implementing our existing vision. In the vision's final form, however, we were already envisioning a facility of 36 quality bedrooms and the dining and catering space in three buildings set widely apart from each other.

During the implementation phase, decisions had to be made on the specific services we would offer at what price. Programs had to be designed and developed; marketing strategies and tactics evolved; and promotional materials developed and used. There were extensive renovations to plan for, and to quality and safety levels that would permit us to host the groups we wanted to attract.

As an important step toward our ultimate vision, we established a new organization, "The Strathmere Centre for Management and Organizational Development," distinct from our hospitality services but potentially a strong client for them. We channelled my own workshops and seminars through the Centre, to provide Strathmere with a new income stream.

Catering and administrative services had to be put in place and over time the required extensive renovations completed to obtain a liquor licence. There were banking arrangements to establish, an accountant to retain, and financial accounts to be set up and kept. A legal base had to be placed under the business. Provisions had to be made for managing ongoing operations, permanent and part-time staff hired and trained, and furnishings and equipment to buy or lease. Then, too, the grounds and gardens required extensive work, and parking lots had to be built – and all of this and more to be carried out under challenging financial circumstances.

A pre-Confederation house the pioneering Phelan family had built over the five years from 1860 to 1865 had long been in need of new wiring, new plumbing, a new well, repainting throughout, re-pointing the exterior walls, a new roof, and such commercial essentials as fireproofing including adding a fire escape from the second floor. The heating system consisted primarily of a large wood stove in the living room and a couple of smaller wood stoves. Throughout the period Alex owned Strathmere, the back of the house had to be closed off during the winter months, leaving only the upstairs bathroom with heat; a descendant of the Phelan family who also lived in the house slept there during the cold months. Liking the view from the original parlor, the Sims had converted it into a country kitchen; what had been a pre-Confederation ceiling had fluorescent lights across it, and a beautiful oak floor was covered with linoleum.

All in all, we could see a formidable amount of work just to renovate Strathmere House itself. For close to 18 months we worked on improvements, which meant we lived in the middle of disruption for what must have seemed to Barbara a long time. Yet, even knowing all this was ahead, I can recall being stretched out on an old couch, the only piece of furniture in what would become again a truly-beautiful, historic and gracious living room, and feeling a deep sense of restful warmth emanating from throughout the house.

Historic houses can be treasures to own but challenging to renovate – and especially if they are to become income generators in a competitive hospitality market. Although Strathmere House was huge, as houses go, there were only four bedrooms, which was much too small a number to serve as the base for delivering Centre workshops and related hospitality services.

Within the footprint of the house, however, there was room for six additional bedrooms: four above the main floor of the attached Carriage House, and two where servant quarters had been planned but never built. Needing to join the new Carriage House bedrooms to the front of the house, we built a corridor above the house sunroom and, when doing so, widened the new space containing the corridor to incorporate two additional bedrooms with a shared bathroom.

All of this gave us a new level of 12 Strathmere House bedrooms, sufficient to move into small residential events. The historic one-room schoolhouse was on the property close to Strathmere House. After placing it on a concrete foundation we converted it into a six-bedroom annex. We continued to develop the facilities until we had a total of 36 bedrooms and the dining and catering capability for hosting privately and effectively three separate weddings and other catered events at a time. In parallel with such facilities development we up-graded the parking, lawns and gardens to create an attractive and functional overall outdoor setting for our development.

A special feature of Strathmere House was the attached Carriage House, with its door into the main house and its sloping concrete floor to facilitate passage through the Carriage House for the Phelan family's horse and carriage. Doing much of the work ourselves, we converted the Carriage House into an attractive management workshop and lecture room that doubled on weekends as a wedding site. Using a large jack-hammer we broke up the sloping floor, and hastily brought in a competent concrete contractor when we found the beautiful stone Carriage House walls rested only on loose beds of field stone without concrete footings.

The interior walls of the house were of the original plaster, on wooden strips, and in the many places where the plaster had deteriorated we stripped the walls down and finished each room with drywall.

In such ways we renovated Strathmere House in a manner that was sensitive to its history, rather than restoring it. The cost of historically-accurate restoration would have been prohibitively high.

To generate the funds required to shore up an undercapitalized business I had to become even more active as a management workshop leader and consultant. This, plus my ongoing university role and my new role as the head of Strathmere Centre, left me less time than I would have liked for creative entrepreneurship.

In previous entrepreneurial ventures I had been at their heart, immersed in the challenges of moving them ahead and functioning as a major component of the entrepreneurial glue that held them together in strong pursuit of a clear vision. With Strathmere I functioned much more at the periphery of the venture once I had negotiated the purchase of the property and established the Management Centre. My primary responsibilities were to lead in laying out our vision and strategic directions, mobilize the start-up resources, and help ensure official civic approvals for the major steps we planned to take.

From start-up our daughter Liz was Strathmere's Executive Director for five years and following Liz, our daughter Mary worked at the centre of the process, as the top managers Strathmere needed. Thankfully both turned out to be exceptionally-competent managers so that Strathmere did move ahead, year by year, with my own involvement continuing to be limited largely to entrepreneurial intervention when this proved to be required.

Phase 9 Settling the new organization down and refining it in action

With the conclusion of the lengthy implementation phase there was a new organization in place. It was identifiable as such, with its own vision, plans, organizational structure, resource base, rudimentary controls, communication processes, and ways of representing itself internally and to the world outside the organization, with which it necessarily interacted.

The complexity of this depended strongly on what sort of an organization we had created. With the organization in its earliest form, we faced the challenge of developing it further and settling it down, giving it the opportunity to take more solid shape. Tasks we had avoided while putting the organization in place had now become matters of some urgency. These included consolidating Strathmere's legal base; refining its financial processes; ensuring that staff had tighter position descriptions by writing and using accountability contracts; developing and formalizing strategic and operational plans; attending to challenges of corporate image; strengthening client service arrangements; reviewing our service lines; establishing appropriate compensation arrangements – and on and on through all the refinements we discovered we needed once we had the organization in place and delivering its services.

We had started out on the Strathmere venture in strongly entrepreneurial mode, with too little attention to what would later become vital managerial concerns. Everything revolved around us, personally, as we held the venture together and led in propelling it forward. It was our success as entrepreneurs, however, that caused the managerial challenges to emerge. The more the organization began to take shape, the more the need to move into managerial mode became evident.

Organizations are brought into being via the entrepreneurial process. Once they exist in early form there is a pressing requirement to employ managerial skills in fleshing them out, settling them down, and refining them in action. It is too early in the process of organization building to have the entrepreneur move out of the process. Entrepreneurial skills are needed until the organization is well established; only then can we safely move away from the lead entrepreneur role. It is not too early, however, to focus more carefully on the managerial challenges noted above.

Phase 10 Adapting the Vision to the Reality Encountered

We discovered, early in our growth, that Strathmere was an exceptional wedding venue. We became well known for the quality of the weddings we hosted, and developed this line of business to include event planning and management as well as the provision of accommodation and catering services. It was a small additional step to make these same services available to management conferences, workshops and seminars organized by groups other than ourselves.

Three years into the venture our daughter Mary and her husband Mike invested the sizeable funds required to become a licensed facility, and this moved us actively into banquets, summer barbecues and corporate meetings. It became clear around that point that we were settling into firm organizational shape under Mary's leadership, and as a family business. There was a Strathmere brand and a recognition factor, confirming us as an enduring organization in the volatile hospitality services market.

The obverse of this settling down was that, at least for some considerable time extending over many years, we stepped back from seeking to create a world-class management centre delivering a rich array of learning services and incorporating a futures focus. Interestingly, in the way environments change and compel complementary changes in proactive organizations, the futures movement ran its course around the world during this period. Statements concerning the creation of a world-class futures centre disappeared, therefore, from our strategic plans.

This move away from the original vision was fostered in important part by the fact that the responsibility for managing Strathmere passed first to Liz, and then to Mary when Liz began a career as a teacher. What they saw in their minds' eyes was not what I saw in mine. Each grew to love Strathmere for its hospitality possibilities and, understandably, moved it in that direction by the decisions they made on a day-to-day basis.

It is an intriguing aspect of organization-building that the vision powering the initial move toward creating the organization can be altered and even supplanted through the accumulation over time of such pragmatic, incremental, day-to-day decision-making. Having set aside the futures centre permanently, and the management centre temporarily, we could then consolidate around the hospitality services niche.

Under Mary's leadership, functioning very much as an intrapreneur, Strathmere has continued to grow as the family organization originally envisioned. It is now a physical facility of outstanding quality as a strong existing base from which expansion may take place. Should this occur, the period of consolidation that followed the initial entrepreneurial process through which Strathmere was acquired and positioned will be followed by a second, challenging and rewarding round of creative entrepreneurship. This may, indeed, be already taking place as we find Strathmere moving further ahead with steps toward re-positioning itself as a professional health and wellness centre complete with an especially attractive Spa, alongside and building from the proven excellence of its established hospitality services and related buildings.

CHAPTER FIVE
The Entrepreneurial Mind and Spirit

The aim of this Chapter is to address how heredity and experience may combine to prepare us at a most basic level for entrepreneurship. For the purposes of the Chapter, I have assumed you are strongly motivated to become a creative entrepreneur and can see yourself engaging in the sorts of activity described in the stories. It is highly likely that the fields in which you see yourself becoming active, of course, will be different from mine; creative entrepreneurs active in every social and economic sector search out their own special niches. I will assume, further, that you have the ability to work hard and have been blessed with intelligence.

Granting these assumptions, the question arises: "Can any highly motivated, hard-working, intelligent person become a creative entrepreneur?" The simple answer is an emphatic "No!" In addition to motivation, industry, and intelligence, important though these are, successful performance requires a set of personal attributes combining into a distinctive entrepreneurial mind, spirit and core competencies.

When we explore the possibilities of investing in an entrepreneurial venture, we need to focus on two complementary sets of factors.

First, we seek to determine whether the venture we are exploring has a decent chance of succeeding in its marketplace in light of its performance history (if any) and its income-generating strengths. These strengths are a composite of such core performance factors as financing requirements and strategies, market-relevant products of appropriate quality, the health of target markets, the strength of its resource base and especially its personnel and technology, existing and prospective competitors, and marketing strategies and strengths.

Second, in parallel and while assessing performance prospects, we need to look at our own entrepreneurial strengths and commitment as prospective entrepreneurs. Even the most promising performance ideas need people of a special mind, spirit, strength of commitment and venture-relevant capabilities for their realization.

Are you a self-starter and self-reliant? Are you comfortable with risk and able to manage it well? Can you handle considerable complexity in your life and do you enjoy confronting it? Have you taken on challenges others have found daunting and learned how to assess and handle them so that those you do take on are usually, although not always, addressed successfully – and have you found yourself able to move on positively beyond failure? If so, you are already displaying some of the attributes essential to successful entrepreneurship.

Entrepreneurial Attributes

Following is a detailed list of fifteen attributes I believe combine into the rich amalgam that forms the entrepreneurial mind, spirit, and related core competencies. To meet entrepreneurial challenges successfully, we need in adequate measure a number of personal attributes.

Before addressing these attributes in detail, however, I believe three cautionary notes are in order.

First, the attributes noted appear to set a high performance standard for successful entrepreneurship. This was intentional, given the special challenges entrepreneurship poses. Yet each attribute is a broad continuum, ranging from weaker to stronger. Because entrepreneurial ventures differ greatly in the demands they make on the various facets of entrepreneurial capacity, the measure we have of a particular attribute could be adequate for certain initiatives but not for others.

Second, although each is first described in positive terms, qualifying factors are then identified for most attributes. Each attribute brings with it challenges against which we need to be on our guard – as, for example, when tough-mindedness carried too far becomes destructive obsession.

Finally, although attributes are presented as an inherent part of the person we have become by a particular point in our lives, virtually all can be strengthened or sharpened through experience, education, and training and development, provided there is a robust core around which to build. We can initially be comfortable with risk to a certain level, for example, and grow in our risk-taking capacity and learn to manage risk better.

The Fifteen Attributes

1. A Strong Achievement Orientation, linked to Self-Reliance

This manifests itself in a higher-than-normal drive toward achievement, linked to possession of a strong ego and, frequently, a capacity to work hard for long periods. If we possess this attribute we will be relatively comfortable taking on challenges and may have sought them out deliberately, in anticipation that we can handle them capably. Underlying this is what one writer calls self-efficacy, which he describes as a high level of confidence in our ability to accomplish what we set out to achieve. This confidence stems from previous success experiences which built and strengthened our self-confidence (Bandura, 1977). If we are not attracted by challenges and have a low sense of self-efficacy, we are less likely to move on a challenging entrepreneurial opportunity should one be identified.

If we are strongly motivated toward achievement – and realistically so because we have proven to ourselves we are achievers – it follows that we will have strong egos. By this I mean, in part, the sense of self-efficacy already noted. In part, also, I mean having a solid sense of who we are that is not easily disturbed by adversity, criticism, outside pressures and the like.

Although open to new insights and ideas which may conflict with our own, we have a level of self-confidence that allows us to trust our judgement even against the collective wisdom of others, so that we are able to forge ahead in meeting inevitable tight deadlines without the loss of time and the lessening of confidence that comes with vacillation.

Perhaps linked centrally to the strength of our achievement orientation, also, is a capacity to work hard for prolonged periods.

2. A Comfort Level with Risk and the Capacity to Take Risks Prudently

Given the nature of creative entrepreneurship, we have to be comfortable with risk and be competent in managing it. When we set out on entrepreneurial ventures, we cannot know in any complete sense how a venture will unfold in uncertain entrepreneurial environments. Then there will be such concrete instances as putting at risk everything we own to secure needed capital, or going ahead on the basis of financial projections with a high level of uncertainty built into them.

Somewhat paradoxically, even though having a high comfort level with regard to risk, experienced entrepreneurs will go to considerable lengths to remove as much of a venture's inherent risk as they possibly can. We did this in the case of Strathmere by using the approach of securing the property we needed through purchasing an option to do so, and then moving over two years to the point where we were prepared to buy it. Yet, after taking care to remove whatever risk we feasibly could, there remained a residue of unavoidable risk we assumed willingly.

A capacity to take risks may be linked in some way to courage, which Greek philosopher Aristotle saw as the second most fundamental of human values preceded only by honor. A more contemporary writer than Aristotle is Rollo May, who has asserted that it takes courage to create in any area of endeavor (1994). Entrepreneurship is a creative endeavor.

In terms of managing risk, the downside to having a strong risk-taking propensity is that we are likely, at times, to downplay prudence for the joy of the risk. Then, too, to manage risk effectively we require the skills to calculate the level of risk with some care and determine whether the prospective benefits from successful action make the risk worth taking. Yet even the acquisition of strong risk management skills and experience will not convert risks into certainties, and we can err greatly in working out the risk/benefit equation.

Another significant concern is that when our risk-taking propensity is linked to strong leadership capabilities, we tend to attract others to our projects who lack our level of comfort with and capacity to handle risk. That is why today, when entrepreneurs approach others to participate in their ventures, it may be a legal requirement and an even stronger moral one that we identify and communicate the risks involved to prospective investors, as clearly as feasible.

3. Equanimity in the Face of Failure and Success

Equanimity is used normally to imply mental composure and evenness of temper in the face of misfortune. Yet it is crucial to a successful entrepreneurial career that we face good fortune with equal composure. We need the capacity to move with equanimity in the face of both failure and success.

The more complex the ventures we tackle, the greater the likelihood that some of our decisions will lead to negative outcomes. We will have "failed," therefore, and perhaps disastrously. Yet, if we are blessed with an entrepreneurial mind and spirit – and, within this, equanimity – we will be prepared for and can accept failure as part of the process. This means, of course, that we see the failures and even major disasters as the entrepreneurial challenges and growth experiences they have become. We move then to address them as such, provided they have not caused us to re-evaluate our vision and commitment – as they might.

Because we are creative entrepreneurs, moreover, we expect to succeed. When we do, it is a joyous experience but may not be an earthshaking event or an especially laudable triumph. In my own case there has always been, instead, primarily a sense of closure. When a venture moves beyond its entrepreneurial phase to become an established, productive organization or reorganization, we have already seen the success in our mind's eye and revisited it regularly as the venture proceeds. When the vision is realized, finally, there is plenty of satisfaction with the fact that it was realized, yet it is no longer the focus of our strong achievement orientation, our risk-taking propensity, or our creativity. Accordingly, rather than resting on our laurels we move on to whatever challenging experience next engages us.

In some rather odd way, and perhaps a peculiarity of the entrepreneurial mind, we do not see either failure or success as they normally appear to be seen. We take success and failure in stride, as two probabilities we know we may well encounter as entrepreneurs.

Underlying the ability to live well with success and failure are three additional entrepreneurial attributes: resilience, flexibility, and the willingness to settle for less-than-perfect results. We need resilience because we move into challenging environments for which there is no proven path to follow and for which, for most of us, nothing in our formal education, training and development will have prepared us. This means it is highly likely that, given the risks we are taking and the inability to be always correct in our decisions, we will take wrong paths so that we will end up with disappointing results at times. Resilient entrepreneurs will accept such events as the temporary setbacks they often are, however, and search out new paths they should be taking. It is then that our flexibility will be called into play as a necessary complement to resilience as it governs the ease with which we are able to regroup and change direction when it is clear we should.

Even while valuing excellent performance, successful creative entrepreneurs are not perfectionists. Indeed, if you are a perfectionist, stay away from entrepreneurship for your own peace of mind and the peace of mind of those who collaborate with you. We tend to need to move so quickly, in such uncertain environments, that perfection will escape us. We need to be able to settle for "good enough" when that is the best circumstances will allow, rather than strive for an impossible-to-achieve perfection. Accepting good enough when necessary is closely connected with our resilience and flexibility. If plans prove to be inappropriate, for example, no matter how carefully developed, we can change them rather than feeling compelled to stay with them no matter what. Here, again, is another of the paradoxes that pervade the fluid and uncertain world of the entrepreneur. We need plans that are as reliable as we can make them, while knowing they may need to be changed fundamentally or jettisoned as events outstrip them or otherwise render them no longer useful.

4. Visioning Capacity

Not everyone possesses the capacity to see things clearly in the mind's eye. If we have this capacity we should consider ourselves blessed. It is a prerequisite for successful entrepreneurship. If we cannot work things through in our minds before we seek to convert what we see there into reality, we will lack an essential touchstone to guide the action we take.

Inspired visions act wonderfully to energize and focus entrepreneurial initiatives. If new organizations are to be created or existing organizations revitalized, we need the capacity to create exciting visions, commit to them fully, and communicate them effectively. Yet we also need the capacity to change our visions as the initiatives progress, and to communicate the required changes without confusing everyone involved. This is so because especially dynamic change, occurring at times in very short time-frames, is the hallmark of entrepreneurial initiatives taking place in uncertain environments.

Visioning needs to go hand-in-hand with the capacity to dream. Paradoxically, however, we need to dream with our feet firmly on the ground. Our dreams energize us. They raise our aspirations above the mundane and give inspirational content to our visioning. Only if we have the capacity to step back from our dream and confront the real life challenges of converting it into a functioning reality squarely, however, will our visioning and complementary planning be concrete, realistic and detailed.

The downside to having a visioning capacity and the ability to communicate our vision is that a vision is something based on dreams, evolved only in the mind's eye. It is not yet real, may never become real, and at times *should* never become real. Yet it can be a powerful influence on the direction we take. We have to guard against the seductive tendency to want to pursue it past the time when we should be recognizing the need to change or move away from it. We have to guard, also, against letting our personal vision work against needed collaboration to the extent that we become unable to work toward a shared vision diverging somewhat from our own. It is not only politicians who need the art of compromise!

We can have visioning as one of our personal attributes, moreover, while not yet having developed the art and craft involved to a high level. The more complex the ventures on which we embark, the more developed our visioning skills need to be as the initial broad vision moves to become ever more detailed and to be seen in ever sharper relief. A still greater skill level is required, moreover, as we move to adapt our visioning and planning to the changing circumstances we encounter.

Should you still be uncertain concerning whether you are blessed with a visioning capacity, before you head home from work or school try to see in some detail in your mind's eye the route you will be taking, road by road and turn by turn. If you do have visioning capacity, of course, your mind's eye will be able to handle much more complex challenges than this. At times and when your capacity is fully developed, you will be able to envision an as-yet-unreal future in remarkable detail.

Perhaps you will turn out to be another Nikola Tesla (1858-1945), a prolific Serbian-American inventor who, as the story goes, would build a model of a new invention in his mind, set it in motion and then push it to the back of his mind as he went on with his business. A number of days later, he would again turn his conscious mind to his invention and assess wear on the bearings, and if he found a problem, would redesign it mentally until it worked perfectly. Once satisfied, he could construct the invention without plans or drawings! (Pinchot, 1965)

It may be somewhat misleading to write of "seeing" in the mind's eye. I am not certain the mind's eye necessarily sees a visual image or whether, instead, the brain is at work in a still more mysterious way. Many years ago as an undergraduate student, the time I had available to study was so limited I learned to dictate my term papers and have them transcribed by a secretary from the social agency in which I worked. I became sufficiently proficient at this that I could prepare and dictate a lengthy paper over a long weekend, incorporating all the punctuation as

I did so. I have always believed I could see the words in my mind before I dictated them. Yet they were never there on some visual screen. My mind simply organized them and sent them out through my mouth or my pen. So, if you do not "see" your own vision in a literal sense that is fine, provided it is there in your mind and you can communicate it.

5. Tough-mindedness, Persistence and Perseverance

There may be very challenging rough spots in the entrepreneurial process as we drive our way forward through highly dynamic environments. We need a special capacity to *keep* driving forward, even when the going becomes difficult. We need the capacity to persist, to persevere, and to work our way through and beyond especially-tough entrepreneurial challenges.

Again, you will know this about yourself. Are you easily swayed from the directions on which you embark and, once started, do you give up easily? Or, as in the old adage, are you one of those who keep going when the going gets tough? There are many occasions when entrepreneurs have to draw on all their inner resources to confront particularly difficult challenges from which it would be relatively easy for someone less tough-minded to back away. There is a coming together, a coalescing into a coordinated whole of all the required strengths available to us that bear on the challenge being confronted.

During one of my own ventures our architect, temporarily occupying also the position of project manager, moved gradually into a mental and emotional breakdown without our realizing it was happening. He ended up in a psychiatric hospital, at which time we discovered his inappropriate spending commitments had cost a great deal in non-productive outlay and lost us a vital loan commitment so that our financial security was threatened to the breaking point. This was a major setback, and it was tempting at the time to simply give up on the venture.

We needed a great deal in the way of toughness, perseverance and resilience, therefore, to keep driving forward. Perseverance came strongly into play as, for two succeeding years, our accountants advised us we were tottering on the brink of bankruptcy and should stop the financial bleeding by ending the venture.

The cautionary factors in relation to these attributes are, first, that it takes judgment sharpened by experience to know when it is simply not appropriate to continue pushing forward in the face of adversity. A healthy tough-mindedness and willingness to persevere can occasionally become blind, self-destructive, too-stubborn behavior. Accordingly, we need to learn how to rein in our "passion to complete" and to understand the nature of such things as sunk costs and know how to factor such understanding into our decision-making.

Secondly, there could be a serious moral and practical problem in persisting beyond the tolerance of those who have joined us in our ventures and want to see us cut our losses.

This is a tough one to call with any certainty. Tough-mindedness, perseverance and the ability to persist well beyond normal limits are such critical entrepreneurial attributes, and can be so vitally important in turning the apparently impossible into the feasible, that I hesitate to caution against them. Perhaps the answer is to recognize that sometimes the impossible is precisely that, and that no entrepreneurial challenge is sufficiently important to break our hearts over or destroy others and other things we value greatly.

6. The Ability to Commit Passionately – Mind, Heart and Soul

Any entrepreneurial venture about which I have felt passionately has engaged me in all three of mind, heart and soul. It is such passion that moves us to new and higher levels of engagement, involving all our faculties and bringing into play all our strengths. This ties back to tough-mindedness, because frequently it is our passionate commitment that underlies and sustains our willingness and ability to stay the course.

I have acted frequently as a consultant in strategic and operational planning. When functioning in this role I needed to wrap my mind around the client's venture for the duration of my involvement if I was to contribute my professional experience and insights fully. Yet I knew the venture was the client's, not mine. Although my heart and soul may have been engaged to some level in providing planning support, they were not engaged directly in the venture itself. That was never the case with my own entrepreneurial ventures, which required commitment at a much more fundamental level.

One writer describes our emotions as "the motor that powers the intellect" (MacLean, 1990). I believe this to be true but incomplete. There is a deeper, more powerful human attribute than the capacity to engage the heart emotionally. It is commitment of the soul, which is at the very core of our being. If this reads somewhat mystically, search through your own experience to identify when something touched you at the deepest level of your being, so that it truly engaged you beyond mind and heart.

There is a caution I need to add here. It has to do with understanding the necessary limits to our decision-making capacity. Our mind, heart and soul may combine into an especially-strong sense of the rightness of moving into a particular venture or of the action we take as the venture proceeds. The venture touches our soul deeply. It arouses our positive emotions in its favor, and the applied rationality we draw on together with our intuition combine into a reassuring sense of certainty. Yet we could still be wrong in even the most carefully considered decisions we make. This is something we may find out only as we act on the basis of the decisions.

We need to understand and accept that we are necessarily fallible in our decision-making. Any one or all three of the powerful factors of mind, heart and soul can mislead us when we work in environments fraught with risk and uncertainty. If we do understand this, "failures" are less likely to destroy us. We will have the capacity to commit totally, allied to the capacity to withdraw without a destructive sense of failure when events demonstrate we should.

Never sell short the importance of the mind in exploring new ventures or working within them once we move into implementation. Our capacity to think, to apply our intellect rationally and objectively, and to draw on the powerful factor of intuition is involved. We cannot propel ourselves forward driven only by emotional commitment, even when this is powerfully reinforced by commitment of the soul. On the contrary, in none of my other occupations have I encountered so strong a need for applied intelligence at a challenging level.

If you are not a thinker and are impatient with the need to apply your intelligence in a disciplined, persistent manner, stay out of more complex entrepreneurial ventures. It takes a sizeable level of practical intelligence to think our way through the many, often-complex challenges we encounter as we move through the different phases of the entrepreneurial process.

It takes, also, the attitude and abilities of a continuous learner because, in moving through unfamiliar and uncharted ground, we fashion where we go next from what we have learned to that point and from what we can learn or conjecture about where we want to head. Yet, at the same time, we need to factor into our decision-making both heart and soul, so that all three of these powerful attributes are engaged.

Then, too, there is the factor of emotional intelligence which has come very much to the fore through Goleman's work in 1995 on the topic. There are highly intelligent people from an intellectual perspective who perform abysmally when it comes to managing their own emotions or in responding in an emotionally satisfactory way in their relationships with others. It is extremely important in creative entrepreneurship to understand the role emotions play in our decision-making and our relationships. It is even more important to be able to manage our emotions in situations where they threaten our effectiveness.

7. Leadership Ability

You may know by now whether you are a natural leader. By this I mean that, in certain circumstances and at different points in your life, you may have found yourself moving into a leadership role, being accepted in this role, enjoying the challenges of leading, and handling such challenges well. In some manner, without leadership education or development, or any burning ambition to lead, the ability to do so has become an integral part of you.

At its most basic leadership is the capacity to influence the behavior of others to move in directions they would not otherwise have moved. It comes in all shapes and guises. Not every leader is highly charismatic, able to lead people to dramatic new heights or depths. Leadership can be and usually is much more prosaic than this. It is being exercised unceasingly inside and outside organizations, and is necessarily exercised whenever people come together in a purposive way.

There is a vital need throughout modern society for proactive, creative, innovative individuals, who are willing to lead in finding and taking new directions, and inspirational visionaries who can capture and communicate a valued future that is not yet real and inspire others to pursue it. There is a need, too, for those sufficiently skilled in the art of constructive influence to move the reluctant out of their inertia – for the energizers, the motivators, who can inspire others to higher levels of focused energy. These are the empowerers and transformers, skilled in the art of releasing the latent power in an organization, group, team, and individual, and in helping to harness that power toward achieving significant results.

It is easy to see, therefore, why leadership is a valuable component of entrepreneurship. It is as leaders that creative entrepreneurs are able to assemble and transform aggregations of individual human beings into vibrant, vital, purposive, highly focused organizational entities – and entities in which individuals collaborate in the pursuit of clear and clearly articulated visions worthy of their combined effort.

Not every leader is a visionary. Individual capacity to envision the not-yet-real differs enormously, even among the highly intelligent and highly persuasive. Yet there are competent leaders who, although comparatively weak in the area of visioning capacity, can become persuaded of a vision evolved by others and run with it effectively in leading entrepreneurial ventures.

There is a special, deeply-ingrained ability some people possess to understand and relate well to those with whom they need or want to become involved. They have the people sense, emotional intelligence and interrelationship ability to work effectively with a broad range of personalities and occupations, and with people having different stakes in whatever initiative is being pursued and differing in what they can bring to it or want to achieve personally. If you have this ability, it will be of incalculable benefit to your entrepreneurial ventures.

In the building or revitalization of organizations we bring together supplies, equipment, physical facilities, information, technology and, invariably, the people who, in some ordered or structured way, make use of such resources to deliver goods or services. We can be involved with people in the earliest beginnings of our ventures and throughout every stage. Therefore, we need a special ability to relate to others if we are to generate working environments within and around our ventures that are tied to a compelling vision, are purposeful, and exhibit a high level of applied energy and high morale.

As creative entrepreneurs, it is critical that we understand people and have sympathetic rapport with those with whom we need to work most closely so that we can win their trust and respect and are able to reach agreements founded on mutual understanding and acceptance. We need, too, the special ability to convert the apparently-outrageous into the fully-acceptable because, to us, what we are seeking is *not* outrageous. We must be able to communicate this. In such activities we are functioning as leaders with a strong people sense.

Despite its importance, leadership is only one of an interlocking set of attributes vital to effective entrepreneurship. Visionary leaders can develop and communicate visions that prove later to be so far out of touch with any achievable reality as to defy the most committed efforts to implement them. Inspirational leaders can motivate others to move off energetically in new directions yet lack the capacity to guide the venture effectively once underway. When this happens, high levels of energy and resources are squandered with no ensuing results of any consequence and with devastating impacts on morale and motivation. As noted previously, there are also times when a compelling vision too strongly held can be an impediment to progress if our vision cannot easily be reconciled with the vision of others with whom we need to collaborate. The willingness to meld our individual visions into a shared vision can be an essential prerequisite to collaborative action.

Then, too, visions need to be both communicated and managed. They energize only those who evolve them until others come to understand the visions and adopt them as their own. This is rarely a simple process. The understanding of and willingness to commit to someone else's vision may evolve slowly and sometimes only when experiencing its use as a guide to action. The vision itself may need to be adapted sensitively over time, moreover, when the perceived reality guiding the vision at the outset encounters the world as it really is or is becoming. If visionary and inspirational leaders lack either or both of the flexibility to adapt the vision and the capacity to manage what can be a complicated change process, the ensuing results could be extremely negative.

Falling within the leadership attribute is the factor of "likeability," as illustrated in the Echo Park story. I am comfortable writing about this factor even though I recognize it may be perceived as somewhat superficial, even frivolous. It has been important throughout my own career as a creative entrepreneur, and it is certainly the case that we do not all mature equally into personable individuals who others tend to like and with whom they are comfortable.

When we engage in especially complex ventures or a succession of different ones, the range and variety of people with whom we come into contact and need to establish healthy relationships could be large. We need, therefore, to relate well to people from backgrounds that differ greatly in relation to occupation, interests, wealth, social status, values, their own respective abilities to relate with others, and so on. It helps enormously if we truly like people across such variety and if, in general, they find it easy to relate to us.

Important though I believe likeability to be, however, it is not difficult to identify celebrated entrepreneurs operating at a much larger scale who would never be scored highly on this factor and, indeed, are noted for the reverse. Underlying their success are other compensating entrepreneurial strengths.

8. A Significant Measure of Natural Ability in Managing

Having natural leadership ability is no guarantee we will perform well as managers. There are highly effective leaders who have little or no managerial capability beyond the capacity to lead (itself a key managerial competence). The best leaders are forward-looking proactive visionaries who search out the most appropriate directions, inspire others to follow them, and maintain the high levels of motivation and morale during their pursuit that is so vital to effective entrepreneurship.

Yet as lead entrepreneurs, once we embark on a venture we have to *manage* it to completion in a way that is more complex than leadership.

We have to take our broad-gauged vision, for example, and develop it into much more detailed strategic and operational directions. This done, we have to decide on the most appropriate organizational structure and put it in place, with the decisions on organizational structure being interwoven with and complemented by the need to decide on, plan for, mobilize, and effectively deploy the people, supplies, equipment, facilities and technology we need. Our leadership strengths, too, have to be applied managerially in activating all of this – and especially in building and maintaining effective interaction among the people we involve in various roles

Other managerial challenges we must meet include identifying and implementing the controls needed to stay on top of everything we put in place. This includes the performance measurement, evaluation and other information-gathering and assessment processes we need. We have to ensure, also, that the decisions which need to be taken *are* taken, hopefully in an informed, wise and timely way. We also have to build and maintain effective communications of both a formal and informal nature, and pay effective attention to the challenges of representing our venture both inside and outside the organization we are building or revitalizing.

Unless we move into entrepreneurship from years of proven managerial experience, we will have few if any of the professional management skills when we tackle our first entrepreneurial ventures. Most of what we come to know about managing, therefore, will be learned while confronting the challenges of entrepreneurship. Yet what we will take into our ventures, if we have inherent managerial ability, is something akin to an intuitive sense of what needs to be done and a willingness to do it.

We may also take into our managing an entrepreneurial mind and spirit. As achievement-oriented individuals with a propensity to take measured risks, backed by a capacity for sustained effort, a strong people sense, an ability to live well with success and failure, passion, perseverance, and integrity, we will be equipped to at least move on the managerial challenges and learn from confronting them. It is important that each attribute noted in this sentence is also an attribute possessed by competent managers.

If we are more leader than manager, and lack natural managerial ability, does this mean we cannot take on the role of an entrepreneur? In those of my own ventures where I was the entrepreneur and worked without active partners, it was imperative that I started with at least an affinity for managing and learned to manage well. Each venture was, by nature, a *managed* one and there was no one else available to act as top manager. Yet competent entrepreneurs can work in concert with equally competent top managers, provided they share a common vision, are clear on their respective roles, are skilled in interpersonal collaboration, and the manager's greater capacity in managing is matched by the entrepreneur's capacity in entrepreneurship. In some ventures, however, there may be leadership of a visionary order but not the management capability required to cope practically with the implementation of the vision.

9. Tolerance for Ambiguity, and Decisiveness under Uncertainty

Tom Peters wrote of the capacity of managers to thrive on chaos (1991). This capacity is important, too, for success in entrepreneurship. As I understand it, the expression is not meant to imply that, wherever we find a successful manager – and, equally, a successful creative entrepreneur – we will find chaotic environments they have deliberately created and within which they delight. It implies, more accurately, that they have a special feel for the impermanence that is all around us and are at their best in dealing effectively with the chaos inherent in our worlds.

They are able to bring relative order out of chaos because they become particularly alive in dealing with ambiguous, uncertain, complex, difficult-to-manage situations. Such situations call upon their special strengths and they are able to move on them as the challenges they are. They have a tolerance for ambiguity, and the comparatively rare ability to be decisive in situations of considerable uncertainty where it is truly impossible to know in advance the right decision to make.

There is, however, a second sense in which we thrive on chaos. As creative entrepreneurs we do move at times away from stability to create chaotic situations we fully expect will be only temporary. We do so because that is the only way we can see to move from a stable but unsuitable present to a more appropriate future. This is what *intrapreneurs* do, regularly. They see established structures, processes, procedures or technologies they believe are dysfunctional or could be improved in some useful way, and take on the challenge of disrupting them to move away from what exists as a necessary step toward where the organization should be.

At the time we moved into Public Works it had been significantly reorganized over the previous six years, and managers and staff were hoping for a new period of stability. Yet our mandate was to reorganize the reorganization because, in major ways, it had proven inappropriate to a new environment and to a new perception at the highest levels of government of the role the Department should play. We needed skill in handling the chaos we created and to manage our way through much ambiguity and uncertainty. In the three months after leaving the public service I documented our experience during what we had called "Project Renewal." The title of the resulting manuscript emerged very readily as *Organization under Stress.*

10. Creativity Linked to Innovative Capacity

People differ significantly in their creative capacity. If you happen to be among the more creative, this will have appeared in relation to any one or more of the media through which we apply our creativity. You may recall the anecdote about Michigan artist and sculptor John Coppin in the Echo Park story. Working with oils and clay as his media for creativity, he saw – through an artist's eye – that the media in which we were creating were the raw materials out of which organizations are built.

As entrepreneurs we call upon our creative capacity in many ways. These include identifying options for successful negotiating; designing workable deals; engaging in creative resourcing through which we search out new and sometimes ingenious ways of securing and allocating needed resources; designing and developing new products; using physical property creatively – and so on, through potentially every area in which we become involved as entrepreneurs.

In using our creativity, we experience some of the special joy of being an entrepreneur. Yet, if we are not ourselves highly creative, in the sense of being more apt than most to obtain creative insights aimed at resolving problems or seizing opportunities, we can still produce exciting innovations by managing both the insights of the more creative people with whom we work and those insights we glean from what we read and observe. This capacity to transform creative insights into organizational innovation is of central importance to entrepreneurship.

The creativity we are addressing here is a special category – namely, creativity-in-organizations. It may be similar at its core to the creativity of artists, scientists, inventors, and writers. Yet it is embedded and manifests itself in its own creative milieu – the world of organizational growth and development. This milieu is both turbulent and complex. It is one in which the creative scientist or inventor who seeks to fill the role of entrepreneur would be as much at sea as the creative entrepreneur aspiring to be creative in science. It requires the capacity to move creative insights beyond the realm of exciting ideas into that of organizational innovation. It is this ability to move beyond a creative insight into a valued innovation that distinguishes creative entrepreneurs from the creative thinkers who never progress beyond their thoughts and ideas.

11. Integrity, in both its primary meanings

If we are to function successfully as creative entrepreneurs, we need integrity as a core attribute, and in both its senses. First, it is one of the most fundamental values required of us. If people with whom we want to work do not see us as possessing moral integrity, they will neither trust us nor be willing to accept us as the entrepreneur in a joint venture. There is an important sense, too, in which moral integrity is an integral part of positive self-efficacy and of the ego strength we need to drive forcefully ahead in turbulent environments, powered by a belief in our own worth and in the rightness of what we are attempting.

I have not previously addressed in any depth the issue of the obligations we assume as we pursue an entrepreneurial venture. Yet these obligations are numerous and varied. If we have the special gift entrepreneurs require of being able to persuade others to join us in our endeavors as shareholders, partners, financiers, and suppliers, we need to be aware that a trust relationship has been established between ourselves and each of them. They may join us not because they understand the venture as fully as we do, or share our vision to the same intensity, but because we have appealed to them as someone who can be trusted and who is embarking on an exciting venture to which they find themselves attracted.

It has intrigued me, time and again, how the business plans and other supporting documentation we have prepared with so much care have been read in only a cursory way by prospective partners and financiers. Entrepreneurs are storytellers that capture and convey their passionate support for an exciting vision and our insights into the practical realization of that vision. The venture becomes real and attractive because we make it so in our story and because, as storytellers, we manage to convey conviction, commitment, capability and, above all, integrity. This is a gift that brings with it the strongest of obligations to work toward making the story real in the results we achieve.

We will not always succeed in the entrepreneurial ventures we pursue, disappointing investors who place their faith in our entrepreneurial ability. Difficult though that will be, however, we should not dwell on it too strongly afterwards. When people join us, as the entrepreneurs we clearly are, we have fulfilled our legal and moral obligations if we make them aware of the risk factors inherent in our venture and if, further, we commit ourselves heart and soul to the venture's success. We are not miracle workers. We can, however, strive uncompromisingly to deliver against our commitments.

Trustworthiness and honesty can be incorporated comfortably under integrity. There are also the ethical underpinnings of principled negotiating to consider. Win-win negotiating is more effective than either hard or soft bargaining because it is principled in two senses: we search out agreed principles on which to negotiate, and we conduct our negotiating in a principled, ethical manner. There are ethical implications, too, in the extent to which we exercise our special persuasive and negotiating strengths to bring shareholders into our ventures to their possible detriment. As yet another ethical consideration, I noted in an earlier context that it is unethical to leave prematurely the ventures we pursue, and to take ill-considered risks exceeding too greatly the risk tolerance level of partners and shareholders. Finally, although this is not as readily apparent, when we adopt a leadership philosophy and style that is empowering, transformative and participative, we are making an ethical choice regarding how we will exercise our leadership capabilities.

Integrity is also critical in its second sense of being centered, of "having it all together." There is something immensely reassuring to others when they sense or learn that we are at peace with ourselves, possessing cohesiveness and together-ness rather than being a mercurial mass of conflicting emotions and attitudes. There is so much inherently unpredictable in the workings of the entrepreneurial process that it is of great value to have an entrepreneur of integrity at its center who is able to bring a necessary measure of dynamic stability to it. I have referred previously to the entrepreneur as the essential glue holding the many and shifting elements of entrepreneurial initiatives together. Integrity is a key ingredient of such glue.

12. An Inherent Capacity in Win-Win Negotiating

As creative entrepreneurs we find ourselves involved at times in situations where we cannot achieve what we want or need to achieve by any means other than negotiating. Such negotiating is evident in the cases presented earlier.

In the school bus company case it was involved in obtaining a rent-free apartment in exchange for acting as nursery school president and CEO; in securing our first station wagon; in obtaining Board acquiescence to having me provide transportation services; in working out transportation arrangements with parents and other schools; in bringing together a group of qualified drivers, on suitable terms; and in transforming drivers into owners employed under contract.

In the Glendon Park story it was evident in acquiring the property on suitable terms and conditions; in bringing in our first, crucial investor; in attracting qualified staff and our first campers in advance of the day camp being fully ready; and in obtaining credit from suppliers while still unproven as a business. In the case of Echo Park, there were the same challenges of acquiring the property, obtaining investors, and bringing in our first set of students and campers.

Throughout several of the stories, the apparent ease with which I was able to move into new ventures without upfront capital is somewhat misleading. It would, in fact, have been difficult or impossible had I not moved naturally as a win-win negotiator. Because this was not something I learned formally, having at no point studied negotiating or worked deliberately on the development of negotiating skills, it seems to fit suitably as one of the constellation of personal attributes required for creative entrepreneurship.

Hard bargainers set their sights on winning. The harder the bargain, the greater the cost to the other party and the greater their sense of achievement. Soft bargainers who shy away from conflict simply seek an agreement no matter if they have to incur a cost that is unfair to them. Principled win-win negotiators are committed to reaching agreements that are fair to both parties, and in which both sides obtain what they want from it or, at least, obtain what they acknowledge is reasonable and fair, given all the circumstances that emerge as the negotiation proceeds.

Reflect on how quickly we acquired the Strathmere, Glendon Park and Echo Park properties, each at an acceptable price and on workable terms and conditions. We could never have accomplished this had we not worked on the basis of strong rapport with the respective property owners and on the basis also of their comfort level with our commitment, integrity, sense of fairness, and trustworthiness. The people we will want to work with as creative entrepreneurs will always, even if only subconsciously, form an early assessment of whether we are principled individuals who are clear and open about what it is we expect to obtain from the relationship, and whether we are prepared to approach it from a win-win stance.

13. The Capacity to Communicate

This does not refer to communication knowledge and skills entrepreneurs can and should acquire through professional education, training and development. Rather, it is how we normally communicate with other people and, in turn, how skilled and sensitive we are to receiving and understanding their attempts to communicate with us. It is essential to success in dealing effectively with the relationships that are so central to creative entrepreneurship and is the basis on which more formal communication training and development can occur.

As we grow throughout our lives, we differ in how competent we become in handling the communication challenges that envelop us, and how effectively we use the various communication channels to interconnect with others. This includes our ability to use the various electronic, written and spoken media, and to listen to others and understand their messages. It includes, also, tuning into more complex communication including body language within which we find ourselves enmeshed. It also includes communicating, in some still more total way, that we are capable, trustworthy, committed, sincere, worthy of respect – or to our detriment, communicating that we are only some or none of these.

The ability to engage in multidirectional, multimedia communications is a complex amalgam of many things and becomes, over time, a natural part of who we are. As creative entrepreneurs, we call it into being in many different situations: identifying entrepreneurial niches from what we perceive in our environments, reading the signals that tell us an entrepreneurial opportunity may exist; searching out the information and insights we need to establish whether these niches are propitious; building rapport with those we want to involve with us and communicating to them our vision and why we judge it to be achievable; and receiving perceptively whatever they have to tell us, beyond mere words, in relation to their judgement concerning the vision. It is as broad as the image we convey of our ventures and ourselves, and as focused as how well we communicate what we need from others in relation to their specific contributions to the venture. It is difficult to think of instances in entrepreneurship when communication is not at play, and when our communications ability is unimportant to success.

14. A high energy level and strong constitution

Where other attributes coalesce into an entrepreneurial mind and spirit, a high energy level and strong constitution are grounded in our physical side. Yet the mind, heart and soul function within the body and the condition of our body has a bearing on how well we can use each of them. The true amalgam we are applying in entrepreneurship, therefore, is one of body, mind, heart and soul.

If you have been blessed with a strong constitution it will be an important asset to your entrepreneurial endeavors. If you are never or only seldom ill and can sustain high levels of activity without undue stress, day after day over weeks, months and even years, then at least you will be physically better equipped to manage the rigors of fast-moving, demanding entrepreneurial environments and to maintain the continuous forward momentum an entrepreneurial venture may require. If, too, you have reinforced your naturally strong constitution with a commitment to becoming and remaining physically fit through a healthy lifestyle, this will have enhanced still further your potential performance capacity as an entrepreneur.

When a strong constitution and complementary physical fitness combine with the passion of a deeply committed entrepreneur, this produces the high energy level typical of successful entrepreneurship. It is this high energy level when properly focused that contributes to others being willing to work with us and to accept that we just might have what it will take to transform a compelling, exciting vision into reality. It is as if, through the aura of high and sustained energy that surrounds us, we create a drag-stream effect able to move others along with us.

I want to be careful, here, however. I would not want to leave the impression that only physically fit people with strong constitutions and impressive energy levels can succeed as creative entrepreneurs. These attributes do make it easier to tackle certain challenges of entrepreneurship. Yet entrepreneurial attributes operate in complex interrelationship with each other, and high levels of capability in some attributes may offset lesser capabilities in others.

As I was writing this the phenomenal golfer, Tiger Woods, had just had four bogeys in a row and lost a very comfortable tournament lead, going on to win only by the skin of his teeth. When questioned on the situation by an interviewer, his comment was, "My body wanted to move me out of the tournament. My mind, however, moved me back in!"

15. A Sense of Humour

I have very little to write on this attribute, except to assert that it can be a valuable contributor to entrepreneurial success. We need to be able to laugh at ourselves-in-action, to see the humour in what is happening. If we cannot do this, the situations we encounter or create could be very depressing indeed when seen, bleakly, through a humour-less lens.

Conclusion

The core question addressed in this chapter has been, "Has your life to this point prepared you for entrepreneurship, by providing you with a set of attributes which interact and coalesce into an entrepreneurial mind, spirit and core competencies?" Whether you are suited to an entrepreneurial career turns primarily on such preparation – on whether your life has resulted in you having been forged and tempered into a "natural" as a creative entrepreneur, capable of meeting the special challenges inherent in entrepreneurial ventures.

This does not mean you will have everything it takes to lead challenging entrepreneurial initiatives at the outset of your career. Possession of an entrepreneurial mind, spirit and core competencies, although necessary pre-qualification for operating within the field successfully, is by no means sufficient. What it does, powerfully, is give us the mind-set and basic attributes from which to grow as we exercise the art and craft of entrepreneurship. The entrepreneurial process itself, moreover, requires that we be continuous learners. Accordingly, we grow as we proceed from venture to venture.

It is feasible today to make entrepreneurship a life-long career. This would involve preparing ourselves to become the entrepreneur in creating a succession of increasingly more challenging organizations or, in concert or alternatively, to become an expert in the revitalization of organizations. We would take each new organization or reorganization to the stage where its future was reasonably assured, provided we made an intelligent handover to competent managers. Having made such a handover, we would then search out another of the myriad entrepreneurial possibilities awaiting us in the fast-moving environments in which we now live. For those suited to entrepreneurship this could be a wonderful, challenging and fulfilling career, providing the opportunity to draw on and further expand the strengths creative entrepreneurs possess.

It is also feasible – and the route I have taken – to be a creative entrepreneur on a much smaller scale. Following such a path, our entrepreneurial endeavors will find their place alongside or intertwined with careers other than entrepreneurship. Both a fulltime career in entrepreneurship and one that is only of a part-time nature require that we possess the mind, spirit and core capabilities essential to entrepreneurial success.

To complement this chapter, I have attached a self- assessment questionnaire in Appendix 2. Keep in mind that not all successful entrepreneurs will possess each attribute in strong measure – and especially when they embark on their first entrepreneurial venture. The longer we practise the art and craft of entrepreneurship, the greater the likelihood we will strengthen each of the core entrepreneurial attributes. The nature of entrepreneurship lends itself to such strengthening through experience.

CHAPTER SIX
Developing Into a More Effective Entrepreneur

Although I have been stressing possession of an entrepreneurial mind and spirit as the essential core of successful entrepreneurship, there are other factors which support and enrich it. There could be a great deal of room to grow, moreover, in that each entrepreneurial attribute can be strengthened and refined. We can learn, also, to combine the attributes effectively, as for example, when we learn to apply our creativity to improving our negotiating ability.

Entrepreneurship as a Profession?

This is a topic that bears strongly on how we approach preparation for entrepreneurship. What is at issue is whether entrepreneurship should be, is already, or will soon become a profession such as law, medicine or engineering. There are recognized ways of approaching every established profession and it would simplify entrepreneurial development enormously if, once we had decided we wanted to become a professional entrepreneur, there was an obvious route to follow in terms of education, development and certification. The established professions that play important roles in our society have come into being over many decades. Roles that were not originally seen as professions obtained professional status when the following six factors emerged and came together:

1. **Social importance**

   The role became too important to society to be left in the hands of amateurs. Medicine is a case in point.

2. **Definition as an established social role**

   The role became sufficiently well established that it was able to be differentiated clearly as a social role and could be defined in terms of the specific functions performed.

3. **Performance Requirements**

   With the role defined, it could be determined what personal attributes, knowledge, skills, attitudes and values were needed before those who sought to occupy that role were accepted as qualified to perform it at a professional level.

4. **Qualification and Certification**

   Because the required qualifications could be identified, formal provision could be made to develop and certify aspiring practitioners to perform the role. Once certified, they would become officially qualified professionals.

5. **Governance**

   In recognition that required qualifications could change and that a licensed professional could perform below established standards, professions established a governing body. This body was given the right to modify or update the certification standards, pass judgment on performance, discipline practitioners for failing to maintain the standards of the profession and, in extreme cases, decertify a practitioner.

6. **Integrity and Commitment**

   It was understood that professionals would demonstrate both professional integrity and commitment. This required an established code of ethics in light of which performance separated the true professional from the merely technically qualified could be judged.

In assessing entrepreneurship against these six factors, the case can be made that it is as important to society as any existing profession.

There would be something especially attractive about having professionally qualified people working in roles as critical to our well-being as the effective creation and revitalization of organizations. We know what roles are required, moreover, at least to the extent that we understood medicine, teaching and social work when they first became professions. Therefore, it seems feasible to structure formal programs to accelerate and enrich the growth of entrepreneurs toward professional standards of performance. It should be a fairly simple matter, then, to certify people as qualified entrepreneurs, and to create a disciplinary body with authority to pass judgment on the professional and ethical quality of the work of practitioners. Finally, we need professional integrity and commitment in entrepreneurship as strongly as in any of the established professions.

Against making entrepreneurship a profession, however, is its great variety and highly individualistic nature. Moving successfully on entrepreneurial ventures across both the developed and developing world are creative entrepreneurs in every age group, of both sexes, and encompassing people with barely any education as well as those with postgraduate degrees and every educational level in between.

Through their initiatives, such entrepreneurs are adding to the stock of organizations delivering marketable goods or socially valued services. They are free to do so because there is no way we can prevent them from moving ahead if they are inspired to so move and possess the mind, spirit and core competencies of the entrepreneur. Nor would we want to prevent them because no one is able to predict where the next valuable organizations or internal revitalizations are coming from, in advance, and who is qualified to bring them into being.

Some new organizations do come into being deliberately, with considerable forethought, as the outcome of business strategy or public or social policy. One can imagine, therefore, a far-sighted business or government singling out and grooming a special breed of professional entrepreneurs to lead such planned initiatives. The great bulk of new smaller organizations, however, emerge out of some rich composite of factors comprising individual entrepreneurial initiative, creativity, innovation, imagination, ability, commitment, the rightness of the times, the availability of support and the capacity to harness this, and a host of chance factors.

Whatever the future prospects for professionalization, the route is not at present open to us to pursue a disciplined program leading to formal designation as a professional entrepreneur, although we could decide to take one of the programs that do exist to prepare us for working in a particular sector. Completion of an MBA program, for example, will not equip us to move professionally as creative entrepreneurs but will give us a useful background should we wish to become active as a business sector entrepreneur or intrapreneur. There are comparable degrees and other educational backgrounds that could prepare entrepreneurs to work in other sectors.

Should it turn out that we will continue to lack the official designation, however, if we are starting out with the mind and spirit of an entrepreneur we can become more professional in practice:

- We can acquire a comprehensive knowledge base relevant to entrepreneurship and develop the entrepreneurial skills to put the acquired knowledge to effective use;
- We can have the attitudes conducive to entrepreneurial success; and, finally,
- We can approach entrepreneurship from a strong base of relevant, deeply held values that lead and guide ethical entrepreneurial performance.

With this in mind I propose to take these four success factors, in turn, to show what is involved in equipping ourselves to move professionally as entrepreneurs.

Moving more professionally: Four Additional Success Factors

1. Acquiring a strong knowledge base

Each key role in society has its specialized knowledge base which practitioners must acquire if they are to perform the role effectively. Such knowledge is the essence of the sum and substance of everything we come to know from myriad sources that is applicable to the effective performance of whatever role we are occupying.

There is indeed a rich knowledge base underpinning successful entrepreneurship. Much of what we need to know we will learn as we move into and through entrepreneurial ventures. What will tend to set our more deliberately identified learning priorities will be the recognition that our knowledge base is weak in key areas and that this is preventing us from moving ahead as fast as we otherwise might. This means we should be conscious of ourselves-in-action, sensitive to and honest about where we need to grow. We cannot carry out visioning effectively, for example, without the knowledge needed to give our visions substance and reliability. Neither should we enter into a new area of activity without learning all we reasonably can about it in whatever time is available for this.

We can acquire a solid and constantly growing knowledge base in various ways. Briefly, we can learn:

Through our own entrepreneurial ventures, because of learning challenges and opportunities inherent in the practice of entrepreneurship itself. Effective entrepreneurship requires a continuous learning commitment. When no one has been there before to show us the way, we must learn moving forward. As an important success factor, entrepreneurs need to be in continuous learning mode. This is a particularly valuable source of new knowledge, given that knowledge is not fully acquired, consolidated, and incorporated into the body of what we already know until we have had the opportunity to test and refine it in practice.

Through finding a lead entrepreneur as mentor. Before we move into our own entrepreneurial ventures, one way to prepare is to work with a lead entrepreneur and observe him or her in action. I learned a great deal from working with John Macdonald, as the Public Works story reveals. The bulk of what I learned, moreover, was absorbed during our working together rather than through any deliberate effort on my part to learn from him or on his part to teach me.

From fellow entrepreneurs. We can observe, talk with and learn from both successful and less successful fellow entrepreneurs, even when they are working on ventures very different from our own. Although entrepreneurial situations differ widely, they tend to share a common entrepreneurial process.

Through formal education, training and development. Educational institutions at secondary school, college and university levels are taking an interest in entrepreneurship and making relevant courses available. Even if they were not, however, once we understand what entrepreneurship encompasses we will find useful material worth studying in many areas not linked directly to entrepreneurship. There are also many useful professional development programs of short duration to be explored once our personal development priorities are clear.

Through the many books, popular articles and learned papers pertinent to entrepreneurship that have emerged in recent years. These range from case material detailing the experience of entrepreneurs in action to pieces which together, in breadth of coverage, address virtually every aspect of entrepreneurship in which we may be interested.

Appendix Three provides some examples of the vast range of literature that exists relevant to entrepreneurship.

2. Acquiring and Sharpening Entrepreneurial Skills

There could be a long distance between knowing about how something should be done and being able to do it. Students may graduate with excellent grades yet turn out to be incompetent as performers in the real world of organizations.

The specific skills entrepreneurs need parallel, to some extent, the required knowledge base. There is a range of such skills, able to be acquired as we develop into more professional entrepreneurs. However, because there is such a range of potentially valuable skills we can acquire, the same question of priorities arises as with the acquisition of a strengthened knowledge base. Some skills are so basic we absolutely must have them. In this category I would include those bearing on the core entrepreneurial attributes explored in Chapter Five. Beyond these, however, are scarce skills peculiar to the environment within which we are or will be working or to our particular venture. In relation to Strathmere, for example, we needed skills in the development and delivery of hospitality services that would be of little or no value to many other entrepreneurial ventures.

Some of the strengths we require do not fall readily into either the expansion of our knowledge base or the development of new skills. This is particularly so in relation to our basic attributes. These are not strengthened solely or even primarily through deliberate development initiatives, but through growth in the process of successful entrepreneurship itself. For example, experience may lead to a stronger and more focused achievement orientation or to a higher comfort level regarding risk and a strengthened capacity to take risks prudently. It might lead to a strengthened ability to live well with both success and failure; to greater resilience and flexibility; and to the strengthening of a basic tough-mindedness, persistence and perseverance. It may also lead to a strengthened ability to commit passionately and to maintain our commitment once made; to a strengthened tolerance for ambiguity and a greater ability to be decisive under conditions of risk and uncertainty; and to a strengthened creative and innovative capacity.

There is, then, a professional skill-set entrepreneurs should seek to develop, in complement to the required knowledge base. We have to make the bridges from our core entrepreneurial attributes, to a strengthened knowledge base, to a professional skill set, and to circle back to reinforced attributes. All of this, moreover, has to come together into an effectively integrated entrepreneurial capability. It also needs to be intermeshed, in turn, with appropriate attitudes and fundamental values.

3. Acquiring Positive Attitudes

As entrepreneurs, our attitudes are the established ways we think about and approach the people and events we encounter during entrepreneurial ventures. What we have been learning over recent decades concerning emotional intelligence reinforces what competent entrepreneurs know intuitively. That is: the importance to entrepreneurship of how effectively we approach our relationships with others, sensitive to the emotions at play; what attitudes we take to the challenges we face; and, how positively or negatively, we address our roles as entrepreneurs.

One of the most obvious examples of attitude-in-action is the distinction between the optimist and the pessimist. They may be working from identical knowledge bases and equally strong skill-sets but differ significantly in their outlook on life and, therefore, in how they respond to the situations they encounter.

Successful entrepreneurs tend to be optimists. Normally, they are positive, self-confident people who approach challenges in the expectation they can address them successfully. It helps, too, to have a healthy sense of *joie de vivre*, of the sheer joy of living, because this spills over into everything we do in working with people and tackling challenges.

As entrepreneurs we are able to exert significant influence over those working with us on our entrepreneurial ventures. We influence significantly, also, the working climates we create. Such influences can be toxic or nourishing and, as entrepreneurs, we can be toxic or nourishing in our individual relationships. We need to be aware, therefore, of the importance of the attitudes we adopt and reveal, and of which attitudes are positive and which negative in the entrepreneurial environment.

Because attitudes are not permanently ingrained in our psyches we can, as part of our growth, work toward acquiring more positive and more supportive attitudes where these are needed, across a whole spectrum of entrepreneurial concerns. The following attitudes appear important to entrepreneurial success:

Maintaining a balanced approach to money. We need to respect money but recognize it as yet another resource we can put at risk within our ventures. This works in combination, also, with having a conserver attitude toward the resources we acquire, so that we employ them readily but do not spend or assign them in a profligate manner.

Approaching venture-relevant problems as the challenges they are, and being enthusiastic in tackling them. This includes being reassuring in the midst of chaos, approaching chaotic situations in ways that dampen down the confusion.

Approaching our relationships in a nourishing way - aware of and avoiding the negativism, impatience, condescension, air of superiority, lack of friendliness, lack of recognition and the like that are so toxic to relationships.

Having an entrepreneurial attitude to success and failure. This involves us, as Kipling states of meeting with triumph and disaster – "in treating those two imposters both the same."

Being appreciative of the authority of expertise and knowledge but not awed by the authority of position. This attitude helps support us when, as we frequently must, we approach and work with people in authority to obtain the support we need.

Regarding clients and customers with respect and sensitivity and dealing with them accordingly.

Recognizing an unyielding commitment to perfection as the enemy of entrepreneurship. Instead, we approach the results we seek from the perspective that "good enough" can be superb when that is all the situation will permit.

Being comfortable with risk, accepting it as a necessary part of entrepreneurial ventures.

Approaching our leadership in a positive, transformational way: seeking to draw willingly and actively on the strengths of those who are prepared to support us in pursuing our dreams. This requires a positive attitude towards cooperation, partnership, involvement, and participation.

4. Values

Values are more fundamental than attitudes. Where attitudes are settled ways of thinking which influence our behavior, values are the bedrock of beliefs which underlie and shape who we are in a much more basic sense. If our attitude to people we work with is, in general, one of openness and participative cooperation, it could well be because we value people as people and value, also, individual freedom and the right to decide for ourselves. If we are comfortable with risk and willing to live with the consequences, this may stem from the fact that we do not value security to an overly-constraining extent.

The values we hold as entrepreneurs are of both a positive and negative nature. We may value positively each of constructive cooperation, responsible freedom, the right to decide, and ethical behavior. We may value negatively each of hypocrisy, a lack of integrity, and untrustworthiness. We value things to different degrees, moreover – from passionately to only minimally – so that, altogether, underlying our approach to entrepreneurship will be our own set of interacting values of different intensities. Only some of these are crucial to entrepreneurship. The following values, I believe, underlie successful entrepreneurship and are integral elements of its fabric:

Integrity, as noted earlier, in both its senses. We need to place a positive value on honesty, reliability, trustworthiness, and honor in relation to following through on commitments and in our relationships. We should value strongly, also, having ourselves "together," being "centered."

Ethical behavior, conducting ourselves in morally correct ways. The amount of negative press unethical behavior has received in recent years has prompted organizations to formulate codes of ethics, seeking to bring together and state formally the rules of conduct that should govern decisions of an ethical nature. In relation to entrepreneurship itself there are moral issues to which we need to attend on the basis of ethical principles.

The set of values underlying the entrepreneurial attributes: achievement; self-reliance; risk taking; resilience; flexibility; tough-mindedness, persistence, perseverance; commitment; decisiveness; creativity, innovation; leadership; managing; visioning; principled negotiating; communicating ability; cooperation, effectiveness in interrelationships, partnering; the authority of knowledge and ability; continuous learning; action research.

Conclusion

Although entrepreneurship is not yet - and may never become - a profession, we can work toward a high level of professionalism when we perform it. It is necessary but not sufficient to have acquired the mind, spirit and core competencies of a creative entrepreneur; this is the essential base without which entrepreneurs cannot function optimally. Attributes that are so central a part of this base can all be sharpened and focused for improved performance. We grow in major part through engaging in entrepreneurial ventures and learning as we go but in part, also, by seeking more explicitly and in a more focused way to improve our performance in relation to all five of the success factors – attributes, knowledge, skills, attitudes, and values.

We can expand and enrich our knowledge base, and do the same with the portfolio of skills so important to entrepreneurship. We can develop and be guided by those attitudes conducive to effective entrepreneurial performance. And, as true professionals, we can act with commitment, integrity and high ethical standards, as well as ensuring that the other deep-seated values so critical to entrepreneurial success become integral to who we are.

CHAPTER SEVEN
Finding Entrepreneurial Opportunities

In what follows I first provide a list of identifiers by drawing on the ventures described in the stories to show, briefly, how each was identified as an entrepreneurial opportunity.

A detailed account of the search for a suitable entrepreneurial opportunity is in Story Ten, on "Strathmere", where a preliminary idea is converted over time into a clear vision of a new targeted reality. The targeted action that will be required to convert the vision into the new reality is also explored.

Opportunity Identifiers from my Own Ventures

1. Necessity is the Mother of Invention

Whenever you identify a need you cannot meet in any normal way, ask yourself whether it lends itself to an entrepreneurial venture. If you need a nursery school for your 2½ year-old, for example, and no suitable nursery school exists anywhere in your community, so that the developmental needs of other small children in addition to your own are not being met satisfactorily, think about arranging for such a school. If you go further than thinking about it to act on the possibility, you will be moving on an entrepreneurial opportunity.

When I set up a used bicycle business this was a clear case of necessity being the mother of invention. I needed to find money to support my college education, was not allowed to take a part-time job outside the college, had no source of loans, but did have some familiarity with buying, selling and repairing used bicycles and enjoyed doing so. Given where I was, within the confines of a well-populated college, I had a ready market for the services I was able to deliver. All it took to serve this market was to get started.

Many entrepreneurial opportunities emerge in this way. Be alert to the possibilities in your own life, where you need to have something happen yet cannot see it happening in more traditional ways. You will find, even if you have never ventured into entrepreneurship, that it is at times like this your entrepreneurial mind and spirit may become engaged.

2. Identifying a weakness or growth opportunity in an organization with which you are familiar

This is perhaps the simplest of identifiers. Monitor the organization in which you are working, or any organization with which you are familiar, to see whether there is a growth opportunity you can identify. If so, see whether the possibility of addressing that opportunity interests you and you can determine how to take advantage of it through an entrepreneurial initiative.

The school bus company and delivery service originated through this identifier. I had become familiar with how a nursery school functioned, recognized that the children needed better transportation than unreliable taxis, had an excellent part-time driver on hand in the school janitor, and needed only a nine-passenger vehicle to get started. I had no thought of moving beyond serving the transportation needs of our own school. Doing so, however, revealed a market opportunity as other schools requested that we serve them.

3. Having a profitable market niche open up as a result of a venture in which you are already involved

It is not uncommon for one entrepreneurial venture to open up opportunities for others. If you are already an entrepreneur and seeking additional opportunities, ask yourself whether the venture on which you are already working has new opportunities meriting exploration. Glendon Park originated in this way through my involvement with the school bus company. So, too, did the delivery service and messenger service which became add-ons to the school bus company.

At Strathmere, we decided to go into the spa business. It is proving to be as successful as we had believed it might, in part because a healthy Strathmere was already in place and has supported its growth.

4. Chance – luck, fate, good fortune are very much a part of entrepreneurship

The challenge is to identify and be responsive to the opportunities that fate seems to bring us. Echo Park originated quite by chance, linked to some uncertainty at the time over where to go next with my career. Being at somewhat of a loose end, my entrepreneurial antennae were up and actively questing around. A chance encounter was also a contributor to identifying the Glendon Park opportunity. I had not sought out the young couple who brought me into contact with the property and caused me to think about it in terms of a possible nursery school and day camp.

5. A complex set of preparatory factors, predisposing us to identify particular opportunities

Even though the primary identifier may be clear, there can be a complex set of factors in our backgrounds which prepare and sensitize us to the identification of that specific opportunity rather than to others.

I noted, above, that chance was the opportunity identifier in relation to Glendon Park. Yet it was not that simple. There was some complex combination of the following factors which, together, prepared me for identifying the opportunity: background as a teacher; experience with a nursery school; business experience gathered from having operated the school bus company and delivery service; prior entrepreneurial experience that had sharpened my appetite for entrepreneurship; and so on.

I cobbled together an entrepreneurial opportunity from something that really was not there except to a creative entrepreneur. There were too many unproven elements and too many factors at risk for a normal business venture.

6. A "Eureka" Moment

Eureka moments of intense creativity can lead to the identification of entrepreneurial opportunities. This identifier does, however, tie back to the existence of a complex set of preparatory factors such as those noted above. A Eureka moment does not arise in or out of a vacuum.

The immediate origin of Echo Park was such a Eureka experience. That Bloomfield Hills represented an entrepreneurial opportunity to build an upscale version of Glendon Park came into my mind in an instant as we were driving around the community. The experience was accompanied by a strong sense of the probability that I would proceed with the venture. Yet, had I not already built Glendon Park I would not have been in Bloomfield Hills in the first place – and even had I visited it, casually, the thought would never have entered my mind that I might move there and build a primary school, nursery school, day camp, and riding stables. Eureka moments which lead to the identification of opportunities, therefore, can be tied strongly to previous entrepreneurial experiences.

Identifying the opportunity to acquire and develop Strathmere was another Eureka experience. Recognition that Strathmere would be an ideal site for a particular venture I had in mind occurred virtually the moment I drove onto the property.

7. Having our entrepreneurial antennae up and actively questing around

Successful creative entrepreneurs have special entrepreneurial antennae. When such antennae are in active search mode, they facilitate significantly the identification of entrepreneurial opportunities that those without such antennae will not see.

In relation to Strathmere, particularly, there was a sense in which my entrepreneurial antennae were alert. I was searching for a base from which I could operate both a management centre and a futures centre. The opportunity was there because I wanted it to be. I created it in part because of who I was. It was not, therefore, as if someone came to me and said, "Walter, I have the perfect property for building a fine location for your management and futures programs."

Various happenings simply come together in the mind's eye to create and let us see a challenging entrepreneurial opportunity. Similarly, I had my entrepreneurial antennae up and active in relation to Echo Park. This was so because the Glendon Park venture was coming to an end in relation to my role as entrepreneur and the timing was inappropriate to return to university.

8. Building from a prototype

A successful entrepreneurial venture may result in our having a prototype we can put to effective use in moving it into a new application. Through the first venture we iron out the challenging problems we encounter as we meet them. We come to know our venture exceptionally well, have created the systems and processes we need to manage it, have the legal and financial underpinnings in place, and have learned how to operate it profitably including learning how to acquire and retain the quality and mix of staff and other resources the venture needs.

Looking at what we have created, we can see that with care in choosing the next locale in relation to identifying a healthy market, we could replicate our venture remarkably quickly in comparison to how long the first one took to establish. This is, first, because we have a prototype to work from and, secondly, because an existing successful venture simplifies significantly the challenge of bringing together the resources needed to build the next.

In developing Glendon Park successfully we had created such a prototype, around which we built Echo Park. Had I wished to replicate Glendon Park and Echo Park in other suitable communities it would have been a much simpler challenge than getting these first two in place.

Strathmere, also, has developed into a possible prototype. What we have created in the greater Ottawa area lends itself to replication in communities of similar size or larger with buoyant economic climates and a healthy universe of organizations committed to training and development and to holding off-site meetings. One can also foresee there being a market for weddings and other special social events in vibrant communities the size of Ottawa. A key proviso, of course, is that someone has not already moved into the particular marketplace with a similar set of services delivered from an equally attractive facility.

A variant of this identifier would be to search out organizations with the identifiable strengths to support a partnership with Strathmere to enable us to increase significantly our existing income streams and enrich the Strathmere facilities, moving on what now exists from a position of strength.

9. Building from an Existing Base

This is a variant of the previous identifier. In successfully pursuing a particular venture we may find ourselves at some point with an existing base that is strong enough to support opening up new opportunities that were not there, previously. It could be that we have developed any or all of sizeable goodwill, a strong financial base, credibility among those with whom we wish to associate, or a serviced property or human resource base that facilitates moving into a related venture. Echo Park and Strathmere are examples of this.

10. Compatible Complementarity

Awkward though this term is, it describes an excellent opportunity identifier namely, reviewing existing ventures to see whether there are compatible and/or complementary services to add to what already exists. Adding delivery and courier services to a school bus company is a case in point. So, too, was having the same property serve the needs of a nursery school, family recreation program, day camp and riding stables.

Imagine you own a 200 acre historic farm, and are using twenty of its thirty-five commercially-zoned acres for a hospitality services venture. This leaves valuable commercial acreage for other ventures. Think about the possible businesses you might create alongside your hospitality business services, taking advantage of the services the existing business could provide to new business lines and taking advantage, also, of the acreage you own and where you are situated. You can probably think of several new ventures that are fully compatible with and complementary to the hospitality services venture. You may also be able to think about ventures which, although they interest you, would simply not fit with the existing business.

11. Being in the right place, at the right time, with the demonstrated ability to address an opportunity.

Entrepreneurial opportunities do not always have to be found. They can be offered to us because someone has discovered that we possesses the experience, background and mind set, spirit and special competencies that fit the role they want us to play, even if they do not connect these with "creative entrepreneurship."

In relation to York's School of Public Policy and Management, the opportunity came because I was qualified for it and willing to take it on. A need had been identified within the Faculty and given an important priority by the Dean. When I was hired as an associate professor and learned that building the new school had been the basis of a rather weak initiative over the previous two years, it fitted so well with my background and experience it was a natural for me to take on.

Leading the reorganization of Public Works was also an intrapreneurial opportunity offered without having sought it. It originated because, first, the Prime Minister and his advisors believed the Department of Public Works needed to be reorganized and revitalized and gave this responsibility to my Deputy Minister. He, in turn, needed someone he trusted and judged that I had the ability and abundance of energy to lead the reorganization on his behalf and under his guidance.

In the three months prior to being asked by the deputy minister to take on this responsibility I had worked closely with him on major internal challenges. It was the combination of academic background and experience to that point – and particularly entrepreneurial and managerial experience, linked to how comfortably I had been able to function in a public service environment – that had prepared me for working with him so congenially and effectively.

Unless we understand and fit well into the environment in which we are working, we are not likely to see the entrepreneurial opportunities that are around us. Nor, without demonstrated ability in working within the environment, are we likely to be identified as someone who can take on a challenging entrepreneurial venture. I was in the right place, at the right time, with the demonstrated ability to head a major initiative.

12. Upgrading a minor opportunity to a challenging level

There may be something about the entrepreneurial mind which leads the imagination to take relatively minor opportunities and upgrade these to much more challenging levels. The international "Shaping the Future" conference was a case of my being asked to take on the challenge of leading a venture on the basis of proven prior performance. Yet what turned a minor opportunity into a major entrepreneurial challenge was taking the initial request and expanding it into something much more stimulating and demanding.

Growing something relatively unchallenging into a major entrepreneurial opportunity is both the blessing and curse of possessing an entrepreneurial mind. Where others without such a mind may identify challenges that can be handled comfortably in non-entrepreneurial fashion, we see the possibilities through an entrepreneurial lens and – driven and guided by the mind, spirit and core competencies of the creative entrepreneur – move the opportunity to a much more challenging and productive level.

Using Visioning to Sharpen the Perceived Opportunity

Visioning has been addressed in stories in earlier chapters. The vital point in the present context is that an opportunity, when first perceived, may not be sufficiently clear to warrant even a preliminary decision on whether it is propitious, let alone warranting the firm commitment we will later need to make. It is this initial lack of clarity that makes the mind's eye so valuable.

The mind's eye is a wonderful human attribute. Without any investment beyond our time it allows us to build a new organization, virtually. In our mind's eye we can articulate, modify and embellish our vision, dreaming our dreams and walking our way through how we will implement them. We can then test the results of our visioning with others and incorporate the insights this could generate.

Can you see the challenges, potential complexity and vital importance of such an exercise in visioning to finding and considering an entrepreneurial opportunity? It is a question of wrapping our minds around what it is we may want to see in place at some targeted future date. We need to see it in sufficient detail that we can decide intelligently what the venture actually involves and whether, once we see more clearly what action will be required to pursue our vision, we are prepared to make at least a preliminary commitment to its pursuit.

Visioning calls into play an active imagination, the use of creative thinking, and a no-nonsense, hard-headed ability to see things as they are or are likely to become as we create them. The challenge is to be imaginative, creative, forward-looking, prepared to break exciting new ground while, at the same time, having an eye to feasibility and acceptability. We give our creative imaginations a broad, relatively unfettered scope but recognize that if others are to buy into and come to share with us a vision they find exciting they must, at the same time, judge it has at least a fighting chance of being realized.

The initial vision, persuasive though it can be at the time, may not be the vision we pursue ultimately. Yet it is sufficiently compelling that we find ourselves wanting strongly to pursue it. Visioning will have clarified our thinking and developed and shaped further the preliminary insight into a possible opportunity. We will be much better equipped, therefore, to make the needed decision on preliminary commitment.

Even after careful elaboration, however, the vision will not be cast in stone. It is a key aspect of the entrepreneurial process that we adapt what we first envision as we encounter the obstacles, new challenges and new opportunities inherent in an entrepreneurial venture. The vision with which we begin, moreover, will almost certainly be much less detailed than the one which will guide our implementation. We flesh out and fine-tune our vision as we proceed.

When I first heard of the Glendon Park property being a possible site for a nursery school, it was through the young couple wanting to move in this direction. As they spoke about their vision I could envision a large, comfortable bungalow accommodating 22 children, and see also an adjoining, safely-fenced, well-equipped playground. Yet once I had seen the property for myself, I came to envision something radically different. I saw the barn and dog kennels located at the far end of the property from the bungalow being transformed into the ideal site for a year-round venture comprising a state of the art nursery school of some 150 children and a day camp having as many as 400 campers a year without generating an over-crowding problem.

When I took my first potential investor to see the property, the questions he asked as we talked required me to flesh out the vision in greater detail. In similar fashion, as I sought to communicate the vision to other people it began to take on still more substance. After some time – and well before committing to the venture or starting any work – I was seeing the school and camp in my mind's eye as if they were already operating in terms of programming, students and campers, numbers and types of staff, and philosophy. I envisioned what would be our indoor and outdoor equipment, how the two buildings and the grounds would have changed prior to the opening of the school and camp, how far afield I would be prepared to go for students and campers, and what fees I would charge for each of the school, the day camp, and transportation. I also imagined how we would be organized in terms of corporate form and the day-to-day running of the venture, what licences we would have acquired, and so on - incorporating in at least broad outline all the elements of a successful ongoing venture.

The visioning with which we are involved as creative entrepreneurs is occurring in parallel with the visioning of those collaborating with us on the venture. Hard as we try to communicate our vision, what others see in their minds' eyes will be *their* versions of our vision. This requires us, first, to be active in both communicating and reinforcing our vision, adapted to whatever we come to understand and accept of how others are seeing the future end state to which we are all working. Secondly, it requires us to be the guardian of the vision to ensure that implementation action accords with it.

We have to be vigilant in testing all proposed and actual implementation against the future we want to see materialize.

Once we have a clear and compelling vision, therefore, we need the skill to communicate it effectively, so that others can understand it and come to believe in its pursuit. Others need to hear about the vision through our story of what a venture is all about and where we plan to take it, as well our passion and commitment for it. We will be using the vision and its story frequently as a touchstone against which to test any proposed new directions. This will require a strong commitment to the vision, sufficient to support us in pursuing it over what could prove to be a long and challenging implementation process. Paradoxically, we will also be the ones who lead in seeing when the vision needs adapting to new insights, and who lead the subsequent adaptation. As with every other facet of entrepreneurship, visions are dynamic. However compelling the initial vision, it needs to be revisited regularly and updated on the basis of new information, new insights, and changes in values and preferences.

Conclusion

There are many ways to identify entrepreneurial opportunities. For me, the identification of opportunities has always seemed to be entrepreneurial rather than managerial, with systematic rigor only coming into the picture when we are moving toward final commitment. My opportunities appeared to arrive simply by virtue of the fact that I was a creative entrepreneur with the mind and spirit that sensitized me to them. Like beauty, entrepreneurial opportunities may well be in the eye of the beholder. There is a melding of the entrepreneurial mind and the particular opportunity. Both are necessary to produce a genuine entrepreneurial opportunity.

This is not to sell short the considerable array of opportunity identifiers presented in this chapter. Something has to trigger the entrepreneurial response and any one of the identifiers noted above could do that. Always have in mind, however, that the opportunity has to be propitious in relation both to the marketplace and the entrepreneur. Accordingly, we should never embrace the opportunity unreservedly as first identified, no matter how compelling it may appear.

It is too easy to be seduced by a bright idea, by a Eureka moment, or by simply uncovering an opportunity for a new product or service we are confident we could deliver. It is flattering, too, to have someone pursue us with the offer of an attractive entrepreneurial opportunity. Yet no opportunity is worth pursuing, no matter its suitability for the marketplace or how much money it could make us, unless its pursuit will add to the quality of our lives and the lives of those who are important to us.

We need to evaluate every prospective opportunity, therefore, not only from a marketing perspective but from the perspective of our own life goals, other responsibilities, the well-being of those around us, and our own well-being. This requires us to use visioning to clarify the opportunity and bring it closer to reality even if only in our mind's eye. It requires us, also, to step back from the opportunity and assess it against other career opportunities outside entrepreneurship.

Exciting though it can be, an entrepreneurial career is not an easy one. If we have solid career opportunities in other areas – and especially areas which engage our capabilities and satisfy our souls – we should consider these carefully before committing to an entrepreneurial venture.

As a final point on finding entrepreneurial opportunities, some years ago I was asked to speak to a service club group on this topic, and opened my presentation by asking the 30 attendees to raise their hands if they were planning to start a new business any time soon. Virtually all raised their hands. As we talked, I learned they had been meeting regularly over the past several months to explore possible ideas, but had not progressed beyond the idea-generation stage. There was no one among them who could lead them beyond an idea, however appealing, into the clear vision and subsequent required action.

CHAPTER EIGHT
Conclusion

In this concluding chapter I bring together Story Thirteen with some final thoughts about the nature of entrepreneurship and the entrepreneur.

Story Thirteen: The Entrepreneur and the Long Distance Walker

It is the autumn of 2007. Every day except Sunday I walk 12 miles, in three 4-mile segments. Four months ago I was walking 5 miles a day simply to stay fit. What changed was that I decided to walk from Land's End to John O'Groats – that is, from the south-westerly tip of England to the north-easterly tip of Scotland – a distance of 1100 miles when avoiding the highways to travel on secondary and smaller roads. That is a long way for someone who has never walked consistently more than 5 miles a day – especially as I will need to average 18 miles a day if I am not to take forever to complete the walk.

If you are not an experienced long-distance walker, try to imagine walking 12 miles in a day, knowing that the next day you will need to be up at the crack of dawn to do it again, and that a week or two later you will be extending the distance walked simply to strengthen your body and mental fibre. With still more training days you keep adding miles until you can walk over 100 miles a week without discomfort—or at least without discomfort to a level that confirms that your body is not up to the task.

This is not a whimsical dream. I can see in my mind's eye walking through the English and Scottish countryside, enjoying this immensely even while facing the vicissitudes of British weather. I can see myself, also, stopping at bed-and-breakfasts every night to avoid carrying too heavy a backpack.

I have played with the possibility long enough, moreover, that I can see how much I have to do to get ready for the walk besides getting my body and mental fibre in shape. There is a route to plan and nightly accommodation to book. There is suitable equipment to decide on, purchase, try out, and become accustomed to using. There is probably a need, also, to line up a walking companion even though at present I am fine walking alone.

No matter what is required in terms of preparation, the chances are good I will complete the walk. It will not go as smoothly as I can see it going in my mind's eye, because 1100 miles is a long way to walk through strange countryside on the basis of plans made here in Canada. Nevertheless, I believe that whatever comes up during the walk I will be able to handle.

Commentary

Why would I take on such a challenge, and why am I confident that unless something unforeseen happens I will meet it? By this point you should know why a creative entrepreneur might be so certain of such things, even though there is nothing relevant to the building and renewal of organizations in walking 1100 miles. We are proven achievers, loving challenges and having decent track records in completing most of those to which we fully commit. The flipside of this, of course, is that we have a good sense of what we can do. Being prudent risk-takers we do not take on new challenges in a foolhardy way. When we do commit passionately to a new challenge, challenge, however, we are sufficiently tough-minded and persevering to stay with it in the expectation of addressing it success-fully—and we prepare for the challenge to whatever extent we realistically can.

I am not telling you this to invite you to come along on the walk with me. You could be a first-rate creative entrepreneur and still dismiss such a walk as an endeavor with a very low pay-off for the effort expended. What I really want you to ask yourself is whether you can see engaging, not in the walk, but in something of such a level of challenge it makes the walk insignificant by comparison. I have in mind, of course, building a new organization or helping revitalize an existing one. Can you see yourself doing so despite the demands it will make on you, because you will need far more than the attributes I listed as being relevant to my walk if you are to succeed?

The beauty of the walk is its simplicity. It has so few components to it, occurring so repetitively that it is relatively mindless. We walk along, the miles pass, and the day goes by pleasantly – and if howling winds come down off the Scottish hills and torrential rain appears as we walk along the coast, this simply adds new elements to enrich the experience. Once our route is planned and arranged, our body wrestled into shape through training, and our equipment purchased and broken in, all we have to do is walk the 18 miles a day until John O'Groats appears on the horizon.[2]

Would that entrepreneurial ventures were so straightforward! There is no pattern to an entrepreneur's days, no regularity, no simple goals to keep us moving, and no obvious set of skills which, once learned and exercised, will take us steadily forward toward our ultimate goal. To repeat a statement from an early chapter, entrepreneurial ventures can be so fraught with risk, and with so diverse a set of bits and pieces to create and assemble into some coherent yet constantly shifting whole, that they require the mind-set, spirit and special competencies of the creative entrepreneur filling a unique, extraordinarily complex role. Entrepreneurs work to support an organization's growth and stability, keeping everything working together in ways that differ from normal managerial processes. I learned a vital lesson from the financial problems with Glendon Park. During the time I was involved at the heart of the venture, finances were always a challenge and especially early in the project when we were building the revenue base. I could

---

[2] I did complete the walk, covering 1100 miles in just over 18 miles a day. It was tougher than I had anticipated, but the British countryside and the people I met were well worth all the training time and the time taken for the walk itself.

and did strive to cope with challenges entrepreneurially. This meant staying on top of everything continuously – attending to what simply had to be addressed when it needed to be, knowing what to pay promptly and what could safely be delayed and until what feasible final date, and, altogether, keeping everything moving ahead in some form of dynamic stability even if very much less neatly than a well-established enterprise might have done.

If you are functioning as an entrepreneur you will have developed a sense of what is involved in the modern world of the entrepreneur and whether it is for you with all its powerful new complexity and societal turbulence. You could already be finding yourself moving with very little of the capital and very few of the other resources you will need, requiring a special ability to handle pressures coming at you from all sides. There could be particularly challenging pressures from creditors you have earlier been able to persuade to give you much-needed credit to levels not justifiable against the early revenues of the new organization you are intent on building. Chances are you will be building a new organization on your own perceived strength of your future revenue streams and on your skill as a negotiator of credit and other support, rather than on resources readily available to your venture.

Because entrepreneurship is not an established profession, we are neither educated to rigorous professional standards of entrepreneurial performance nor required to work in conformity with such standards. Entrepreneurship is an art, with the soul of a creative artist at its base. It is also a craft, with success resting in some measure on entrepreneurially-relevant acquired knowledge and skills, honed over time through experience or through direct, hands-on learning programs.

I made the case earlier for how strongly entrepreneurship differs from both managing and leading even while encompassing both. The creation of Echo Park illustrates this well. I had led the complex implementation process of transforming the organization we had created until it had in place the strengths required to move out of entrepreneurial into managerial mode.

Accomplishing this required the commitment and skills of the creative entrepreneur. Managing it once in place, however, required the different commitment and special strengths of managers – in the case of Echo Park, the Nursery School and Camp Directors.

The difference between managing and entrepreneurship may be at least in significant part the complexity entrepreneurs need to be able to handle, the ambiguity we tolerate in our decision-making, the flexibility with which we can change direction when change is required, the level of risk we are able to tolerate comfortably, the extent to which we can see things whole while seeing them also in their interlocking details, and in the sheer pace at which we are able to work because of the passionate commitment we make to the particular vision we are pursuing.

Final Word

The imperative need for entrepreneurs in all sectors of society

As society has become ever more complex, organizations have been challenged to become much more effective in dealing with resulting change demands. One result is that a greater value has been placed on entrepreneurship. Burns writes of "a new age of uncertainty; an increasingly complex and changing world in which entrepreneurs have emerged as the species most able to cope with the new turbulence" (2013). If we have the mind-set and skills of the creative entrepreneur, there will be entrepreneurial opportunities as an outlet for our creativity in every sector of society, provided we have the initiative and special attributes of the entrepreneur to search out and address those that are especially interesting.

Let me stress more strongly than I have previously how great a need exists for the creative entrepreneur in the not-for-profit sector and the various public services. It is an absolute imperative of modern civilized societies that we have active, vibrant, caring, and service-oriented not-for-profit and public sectors. As we continue to develop our market-based economies, which pay homage to and reward so disproportionately the successful entrepreneur active in the business world, we are creating a society in which many people are left with social needs crying out to be met. In equally compelling fashion, moreover, our various public services need their own particular brand of creative intrapreneur, able and willing to bring the special strengths of entrepreneurship to helping create and maintain vibrant public sector organizations which match the best of the business sector organizations in their vitality and productivity.

Is Creative Entrepreneurship for You?

Fledgling entrepreneurs are free to move into their entrepreneurial ventures and be rewarded when they do so successfully. Indeed, there is no way we can prevent such entrepreneurial ventures if the creative entrepreneurs among us are inspired to initiate and run with them. But should you attempt it, creative entrepreneurship will bring you more grief than joy if life has not equipped you with an entrepreneurial mind, spirit and certain core attributes. I could train for my walk because the skills it called upon were so few. Provided I trained intelligently and kept my daily performance goals realistic, it was not unreasonable for me to expect to complete it.

We cannot "train" for creative entrepreneurship. It has too many different aspects, calls upon too many different capabilities, and requires so much in the way of a knowledge base and the skills you need to start out on entrepreneurial ventures with the mind and spirit that will give you a fighting chance of succeeding.

You will need to test the option against other career opportunities that are open to you and which are also capable of engaging your mind, heart and soul in the way that, for example, being an educator has at times engaged mine. This means you need to be open to the possibility that you could have in abundance everything it takes to succeed as a creative entrepreneur yet not be motivated to become one.

There is the possibility, of course, that you do not make entrepreneurship your only career but, as I have done, fit it into whatever else has become important to you. This will require that you have the ability to balance your family life, your regular career, and an entrepreneurial venture at the same time.

Along similar lines, it is possible to think of entrepreneurship, in some sense and in some circumstances, as a means to an end rather than an end in itself. There is something you want to see happen that will never happen unless you intervene and, by intervening, you find yourself bringing to bear entrepreneurial competence.

There just might be an entrepreneur within you waiting to be awakened, and you may never know it is there until something happens where your entrepreneurial skills are needed. The entrepreneur in you may be called out by circumstances, even against your better judgment about whether you should become involved. Entrepreneurial capacity is there inside you but is finding expression in other ways. Yet it *is there* and is called upon, aroused and focused by a commitment to meet an identified need that engages you strongly and which requires the mind, spirit and core competencies of the creative entrepreneur.

You may actively seek a career as a creative entrepreneur or intrapreneur, focusing on a particular sector in which to apply your talent. Every sector is a possibility because each needs creative entrepreneurs to help build and revitalize its organizations. The business sector will be the obvious choice for those of you wanting to harness your entrepreneurial capacity to the goal of becoming wealthy. It will also be for those of you who have come to see the valuable role a healthy business sector plays in driving the economy that is so vital to a society's financial well-being. The public sector has the advantage of its several levels, its geographic spread, the great variety of its structured positions, and the well-developed nature of its human resource systems. The not-for-profit sector will be a possible choice for those of you with a strong desire to help meet social service, health and education needs. There are opportunities to explore and needs to be addressed both at home and around the world.

Creative Entrepreneurship is a Two-Edged Sword

The passion that energizes creative entrepreneurs, sustaining us in radiating the forward drive, energy, commitment, enthusiasm and excitement entrepreneurial ventures require, is a two-edged sword. The nature of the commitment underlying the passion can leave us vulnerable to the pain of a major setback – you may recall that John Macdonald's near-fatal heart attack was brought on by such vulnerability.

In deciding whether it is for you, therefore, recognize entrepreneurship for what it is. It has its exciting, fulfilling, service-oriented up-side, giving you the opportunity to exercise every talent you have or are able to develop in the pursuit of inspiring visions and bringing with it the joy that is experienced as a vision becomes a new reality. It also has its downside, and could leave you, at particular points in your life, in devastating financial and emotional shape simply because you committed yourself so completely to pursuit of a particular vision that proved to be unrealizable.

Entrepreneurship is neither safe nor secure. It engages you so fully that you become vulnerable to a catastrophic let-down with nothing left to fall back on except the strength of your character and the richness of your social safety net.

It is far easier for me to recommend that you not leave yourself vulnerable to over-commitment than for you to actually accomplish this. What helps us succeed as creative entrepreneurs is the level of commitment that people see in us.

Psychologists write of "ego involvement" and warn of the adverse effects of too high a level of ego involvement in what we do. That is one of the central paradoxes of creative entrepreneurship. On the one hand, as entrepreneurs we need to commit ourselves so strongly that the inevitable and sometimes extreme challenges do not cause us to give up until all avenues of resolving them have been tried. On the other, it is vital that we not commit so deeply that we cannot extricate ourselves without suffering deep psychological pain and, at times, irreversible psychological harm.

I have been able to contrast, in a stark way, my life as an entrepreneur and in the fulfilling, socially worthwhile role of an educator. I love teaching and am a committed lifelong learner. Yet as a creative entrepreneur for years, I poured the very considerable earnings from my consulting into Strathmere, a venture that was severely under-capitalized. Why did I do so, I wonder, when as a family we could have been living a satisfying life centering on the university and my consulting – both of which were strong revenue generators. In retrospect there might really seem to have been no sense to this. Yet today, from a still longer time perspective, I can recognize Strathmere as the strong revenue generator and satisfying family business it has become, more than repaying any investment into it during its lean years.

The Role of Chance

I have a strong sense of the good fortune that has accompanied me throughout my entrepreneurial career. Almost everything seems to have fallen into place when it needed to do so. Yet with only slight variations in circumstances, there could have been significant setbacks.

In trying to assess what was at play in all of this, I see it as the result of two forces continually at work in support of what I was doing. The first was an entrepreneurial spirit that helped me see the best in what was happening to me and to move back and around and away from setbacks that did occur. The second was that I was truly blessed with a loving family that gave balance to my life and helped me see most entrepreneurial setbacks as minor blips in a satisfying existence.

Engaging the Soul

When I think of the soul, I imagine it as the essential core of who I am as a human being. In my normal everyday life it exists, quiescent, waiting to be activated by something so special as to call upon and require the engagement of my highest potential.

To be engaged "heart and soul" in an aspect of life is to be so fully committed as to involve one's whole being in a manner that transcends normal functioning. It is the polar opposite of what Thoreau describes as "a life of quiet desperation". (Walden, 1854) When my soul is engaged, I am at my most productive and full of the joy of living with an especially high level of focused energy.

There is another aspect of engaging the soul in entrepreneurship when we consider the soul in its more spiritual sense. It was evident in relation to John Kelso and his commitment to meeting the needs of neglected and dependent children.

What was challenging and energizing him when he led in building 55 children's aid societies was a deep compassion for the plight of the children being served. Individual organizations were simply necessary vehicles for meeting the needs he had identified and which had engaged his soul deeply.

Whether entrepreneurship is for you is a personal decision. It will not be a decision driven only or even mainly by logic and rationality. Hearts and souls also have prominent roles to play. I am not sure how you get at this, but you might explore whether creative entrepreneurship would engage your soul. This is an important consideration if, as I believe, our souls are at the core of our being. When our souls are engaged, we are at our most productive, full of the joy of living, with a level of focused energy we are not normally capable of generating. We seem to go into overdrive. Creative entrepreneurship has always done that for me, but there are infinite alternative possibilities of engaging the soul and you should be seeking the right one for you.

For the functioning and emerging entrepreneurs and intrapreneurs among you: may you derive the joys and personal satisfaction from entrepreneurship that have been such a positive force in my own life – and may the universe of organizations be richer through your entrepreneurship.

APPENDIX I
Walter Baker: Career Milestones

1946	Enrolled in St. John's College, York.
1948	Graduated as a teacher from St. John's College
1949	Taught at English High School for Boys, Istanbul (gym teacher)
1950	Landed immigrant in Canada; taught at a one room school in northern Ontario
1951	Enrolled in Queen's University; concurrently, worked as a Social Worker, Children's Aid Society, Kingston Ontario
1955	Graduated from Queen's University: Honours B.A. in Psychology
1956	Graduated from Queen's University: M.A. in Political Studies
1957	Enrolled in Ph.D. program in Political Science at the University of Toronto; founded and directed Courier School Bus Co., Toronto
1958-60	Founded and directed Glendon Park School and Camp, Toronto
1960-62	Founded and directed Echo Park School and Camp. Bloomfield Hills, Michigan
1963	Enrolled in Queen's University, Ph. D. program
1967	Graduated from Queen's; Ph. D. in Public Policy and Management

1967	Associate Professor in Faculty of Administrative Studies, York University, Toronto; led in building School of Public Policy and Management
1969	Policy Advisor in federal Department of Indian Affairs and Northern Development, then Assistant Deputy Minister, Department of Public Works, Ottawa, accountable to the Deputy Minister for reorganizing/revitalizing the department
1974	Professor, Faculty of Administration, University of Ottawa
1978	Organized and chaired an international conference. "Shaping the Future: Canada in a Global Society", Ottawa
1979	Acquisition of Strathmere, a 200 acre country retreat facility, North Gower, Ontario

APPENDIX II
Entrepreneurial Attributes
- A Self-Assessment Questionnaire

When responding to the questionnaire use a scale of 1 to 5, where:

1 =   I do not possess this attribute in any noticeable measure

2 =   I possess the attribute but only at a low level

3 =   I possess the attribute to a decent level but with lots of room to grow

4 =   I score highly on this attribute

5 =   I possess the attribute at an exceptionally-high level

Achievement Orientation

Am I oriented strongly toward achievement? That is, have I found myself throughout my life wanting to take on challenges that many would find daunting, and have I committed to high performance when I take them on?

Risk-taking

Am I comfortable in risk situations, having learned that I manage risk prudently and without debilitating stress?

Living Well with Success and Failure

Do I have the ability to live well with success and failure, seeing them as happenings in the life of creative risk-takers and as possible growth opportunities? As a follow-up question, how do I rate on each of the following attributes?

- Level-headedness/Equanimity
- Resilience
- Flexibility

Visioning

Can I create and envision in my mind's eye, in some detail, future possible happenings and end states, including seeing things that have never existed in the past or present? Do I have the healthy imagination required to support such visioning?

Tough mindedness, Persistence and Perseverance

Can and do I press on with what I initiate, even in the face of serious obstacles, or am I easily swayed from the directions I decide on when others criticize or condemn them? Am I genuinely tough-minded, persistent and persevering in relation to pursuing what I commit strongly to accomplishing?

Passionate Commitment

Do I have the demonstrated ability to commit passionately to ventures I undertake, and to do so in a totally-involved, 'mind, body, heart and soul' way?

Intellectual and Emotional Intelligence

Have I the intellectual capacity and commitment to use my mind in exploring new ventures or working within them once I move into implementation, applying my intellect rationally and objectively and drawing on the powerful factor of intuition? Am I a continuous learner, able to grow from my entrepreneurial experiences? Can I manage my emotions and respond in an emotionally satisfactory way in my relationships with others?

Natural Leadership Ability

At different points in my life have I found myself moving into a leadership role, being accepted in this role by those I am leading, enjoying the challenges of leadership, and handling such challenges well?

A Significant Measure of Natural Managerial Ability

To what extent am I a natural as a manager in the sense of being able to move beyond vision and plans to deliver concrete, targeted results by mobilizing the required people and other resources and ensuring these are allocated and employed economically and efficiently? Am I comfortable and capable in taking on responsibility for delivering concrete results through the results and related actions of other people?

Tolerance of Ambiguity, and the Ability to be Decisive in Uncertain Circumstances

Have I demonstrated the ability to work comfortably and competently in ambiguous, uncertain, complex, difficult-to-manage situations? Am I able to be decisive in situations where it is impossible to know in advance the right decision to make?

Creative and Innovative Capacity

Am I creative, in that I have demonstrated an ability to find creative solutions to problems and challenges I have faced, and to help others find creative solutions to challenges when normal approaches are not working? Can I find examples of when I came up with useful creative insights? When I have had creative insights, have I demonstrated the capacity to convert these into innovative solutions to the real-world challenges they addressed?

Integrity

Am I a person of integrity in terms both of moral integrity demonstrated in relation to honesty, reliability and trustworthiness, and in the sense of having-it-all-together and being at peace with myself?

Win-Win Negotiation

Even without previously knowing the term or having learned the methodology, do I function in negotiating situations as a principled, win-win negotiator rather than as a hard or a soft bargainer? Do I seek and am I able to reach principled agreements fair to both sides?

Communicating Capacity

Have I displayed competence in the every-day business of communicating? Am I able to use different communication media effectively and receive perceptively what others seek to communicate to me? Overall, how good a multimedia, multi-directional communicator am I?

Energy Level and a Strong Constitution

Have I been blessed with a strong constitution, so that I am never or only seldom ill and can sustain high levels of activity over weeks, months and even years? Am I committed to becoming and staying physically and emotionally fit? Overall, has this contributed toward giving me a high energy level to apply to the activities I engage in, and do others recognize and remark on this?

A Sense of Humour

Have I a healthy sense of humour that enables me to laugh at myself-in-action, to see the humour in what is happening to me and around me? Has my sense of humour been an asset in my relationships?

Entrepreneurial Spirit

Taking these attributes together, interacting with each other to govern how I approach entrepreneurial opportunities and challenges, have I shown at various times in my life an active entrepreneurial spirit, manifesting itself in a willingness and ability to take risks intelligently, enjoying and being stimulated by them; to move flexibly and pragmatically on challenges, tolerating a great deal of ambiguity and uncertainty; to live well with success and failure; and to dream freely and imaginatively while also able to turn into action those dreams which attract me?

APPENDIX III
Some Suggested Readings

There is a large body of literature on entrepreneurship and related subjects such as "emotional IQ" and "self-efficacy". The following sets out some of the articles and books that helped to clarify and enrich the contents of this book.

Altringer, Beth, "A New Model for Innovation in Big Companies," Harvard Business Review, November, 2013.

Bandura, Albert, "Self- Efficacy: Toward a Unifying Theory of Behavioral Change," Psychology Review (84)2 1977.

Burns, Paul, Corporate entrepreneurship: Innovation and Strategy in Large Organizations (Palgrave Macmillan, 2013).

Drucker, Peter, Innovation, Entrepreneurship: Practices and Principles (Harper & Row,1986).

------------------ "Our Entrepreneurial Economy," Harvard Business Review 62(1), 1984.

Gauss, Allison, "3 Challenges Unique to Non-profit Entrepreneurs"; available at *www.classy.org/blog/3-challenges-unique-to-nonprofit-entrepreneurs*. (no date)

Gerber, Michael, Awakening the Entrepreneur Within: How Ordinary People Can Create Extraordinary Companies (Harper Business, 2008).

Goleman, Daniel, Emotional Intelligence: Why It Can Matter More than IQ (Bantam Books, 1995)

Gouldner, Alvin Ward, "Cosmopolitans and locals: Toward an analysis of latent social roles," <u>Administrative Science Quarterly</u> (2), 1957.

Levitt, Theodore, "Creativity Is Not Enough," <u>Harvard Business Review</u> 80(8), 2002

MacLean, Paul Donald, <u>The Triune Brain in Evolution: Role in Paleocerebral Functions</u> (Plenum New York, 1990).

May, Rollo, <u>Courage to Create</u> (W.W. Norton Company, 1994).

Peters, Tom, <u>Thriving on Chaos: Handbook for a Management Revolution</u> (Harper Perennial, 1991).

Pilzer, Paul Zane, <u>The New Wellness Revolution: How to Make a Fortune in the Next Trillion Dollar Industry</u> (Wiley, 2007).

Pinchot, Gifford, <u>Intrapreneuring: Why You Don't Have to Leave the Corporation to Become an Entrepreneur</u> (Harper & Row, 1985).

Pinchot, Gifford and Pellman, Ron, <u>Intrapreneuring in Action - A Handbook for Business Innovation</u> (Berrett-Koehler, 1999).

Tidd, Joe and Bessant, John, <u>Managing Innovation: Integrating Technological, Market and Organizational Change</u>, (Wiley, 2013).

www.ingramcontent.com/pod-product-compliance
Lightning Source LLC
Chambersburg PA
CBHW070859160726
48004CB00003B/1150